SECRET
OXFORD

Andrew Sargent

AMBERLEY

Acknowledgements

The author would like to thanks his wife for her constant support.

The author wishes to acknowledge his debt to the numerous books and articles he read while researching this volume.

He would also like to thank the editorial team at Amberley.

Apart from the image on page 65, these photographs are all copyrighted to Andrew Sargent.

First published 2016

Amberley Publishing
The Hill, Stroud
Gloucestershire, GL5 4EP

www.amberley-books.com

Copyright © Andrew Sargent, 2016

The right of Andrew Sargent to be identified as the Author of this work has been asserted in accordance with the Copyrights, Designs and Patents Act 1988.

ISBN 978 1 4456 4782 1 (print)
ISBN 978 1 4456 4783 8 (ebook)

British Library Cataloguing in Publication Data.
A catalogue record for this book is available from the British Library.

Typesetting by Amberley Publishing.
Printed in Great Britain.

Contents

1. Dreaming Spires

Oxford is a dream. It is a city of secrets. The old colleges present blank walls to the street, their honey-coloured stone glowing in the sunlight. Behind them, apparently sheltered from the storms of twenty-first-century life, is a world of mystery. A tantalising glimpse through a forbidden gateway reveals venerable old buildings around a pocket handkerchief of neatly mown grass. Students clutching piles of books or earnestly chattering pass proprietorially in and out past the sign which reads 'The College is CLOSED to Visitors'. Perhaps a stern porter in dark suit and bowler hat stands outside his gate lodge, hands clasped behind his back, waiting to pounce on any infraction of the rules. All oozes peace, tranquillity, tradition, learning and privilege, especially on a glorious summer's day.

The poet and educationalist Matthew Arnold created one of the more enduring mental images of Oxford as a town of 'dreaming spires'. The view from Boar's Hill across the river was his inspiration:

> And that sweet City with her dreaming spires
> She needs not June for beauty's heightening.
>
> (*Thyrsis*, 1865)

The poem, and even the couplet, are largely forgotten, but the phrase 'dreaming spires' lives on.

What the visitor expects, the visitor sees. But look harder. Oxford is far from being just a stage set for the university. Sir John Betjeman, himself briefly an undergraduate (failed) at Magdalen College, identified three different Oxfords. The first and oldest he characterised as 'Christminster', a sleepy West Country market town with its cathedral, a place of markets, farmers and clerics, the sort of place Thomas Hardy wrote about in *Jude the Obscure*. Second, the university as a private place of tradition, learning and privilege. Third, what he termed 'Motopolis', the industrial sector of East Oxford centred around William Morris's car factory. Tourists never venture there.

Betjeman wrote in the years before the Second World War. Since then, Britain has changed and Oxford with it. The Christminster he recognised has vanished, to be replaced by a retail and business centre similar to any in the south of England, with the usual ever-growing ring of suburbs. The university has weathered a storm of change and, although superficially little altered, is now a very different beast – like a swan, placid above the water but working hard out of sight. The industrial sector has continued to expand and develop, bringing prosperity and employment to the city.

Yet Oxford has fared better than most towns. With patience, the bones of its earlier incarnations can still be traced: its street plan is Saxon. Venerable and beautiful college and university buildings are dotted around like gems, some brazenly facing the main

Glimpse of a hidden world. Mowing a college lawn.

The dreaming spires of Oxford from the vantage point of Boar's Hill.

A quiet collegiate corner.

thoroughfares, others coming as a pleasant surprise around a bend down a narrow lane. A hint of the monastic still hovers over the city – and did so even more in the days of the single-sex college. The heart of the city also has more than its fair share of green spaces to refresh both eye and soul: college gardens (sometimes open to visitors), Magdalen Deer Park, the Botanic Garden, Christ Church Meadow, the University Parks, college playing fields, and further out the expanse of Port Meadow. The geography of the town, squeezed between two unpredictable rivers, has ensured that. As you walk its streets, its history is preserved in the archaeology sealed by tarmac and paving stones, and in old houses and shops buried behind modern facades. Only occasionally do the old bones poke through. The visitor – and most residents – quite literally only skim the surface.

The private life of the colleges is hidden away so it is easy, depending which novels you have read, to imagine scenes of anachronistic privilege secure behind those ancient gates. In truth, the final vestiges of that approach to the academic life were all but snuffed out by the First World War. Today feasts are rare and funded by superannuated bequests from well-meaning alumni, rather than daily and paid for out of a bottomless purse. However, there are recondite traditions unique to each college – for example, the Mallard Ceremony at Magdalen! And the university talks in code – at least it has (largely) given up speaking in Latin. Its terms are Michaelmas (autumn), Hilary (spring) and Trinity (summer). Its officers include Proctors and Bulldogs, and it manages its finances via the University Chest. Its colleges have their own flags. Even its costume is colour coded, the smallest detail trumpeting the wearer's status to the *cognoscenti*. During the exam period you may spot

Oxford rooftops looking south from the tower of St Michael's church. The white cupola is on the roof of the Sheldonian Theatre and the large dome is the Radcliffe Camera.

This row of seventeenth-century houses in Turn Again Lane was rescued and restored by the Oxford Preservation Trust.

undergraduates dressed formally in 'subfusc', the dark suit and white bow tie (vestiges of morning dress), gown and mortar board, and perhaps a floral button hole, which tradition still requires when a gentleman sits a university exam. If you are still more fortunate, you might perhaps glimpse a university procession clad in brightly coloured hoods and gowns.

Despite – or perhaps because of – all this, Oxford has produced twenty-six British prime ministers, as well as numberless leading scientists and other academics, saints and clerics, royalty, politicians, famous names from literature and the arts, and notable townsfolk, not to mention much-loved characters from fiction. So many have walked these streets.

Oxford is famously a town of bicycles. In 1938 19,200 bicycles a day crossed Magdalen Bridge, making it the busiest place for cycles in the world. Numbers have declined in recent years as the traffic has become more dangerous. Oxford is also a place of rowers. Despite decades of British Olympic success, there is still only one Boat Race. It is also a town of bells. Betjeman eulogised over the distant sound of bells heard on the river. Colleges, churches and clocks all chime the hours or toll for chapel or meal times in two dozen separate colleges. Each evening the great bell at Christ Church is tolled 101 times, once for each member of Wolsey's foundation – originally the curfew for all students of whichever college or hall. It tolls at 9:05 p.m. because Oxford lies 1°15' west of Greenwich – such is the power of tradition and the exactitude of the collegiate mind.

It is a city of music. Buskers play on the streets while hidden pubs tucked away down dark lanes advertise live music. The standard of student music-making is usually of the highest. In term time, and particularly in the summer, there can hardly be a day when a concert cannot be heard in some college or other. In addition, evensong in college chapels and at the cathedral is usually open to any who wish to attend; a notice may be posted at

Oxford is a town of bicycles.

Right: Rowing down to the start of a race.

Below: A college's rowing triumphs proudly recorded on a wall in coloured chalks. The Torpids are raced in the spring. From a staggered start, the idea is literally to 'bump' the boat in front.

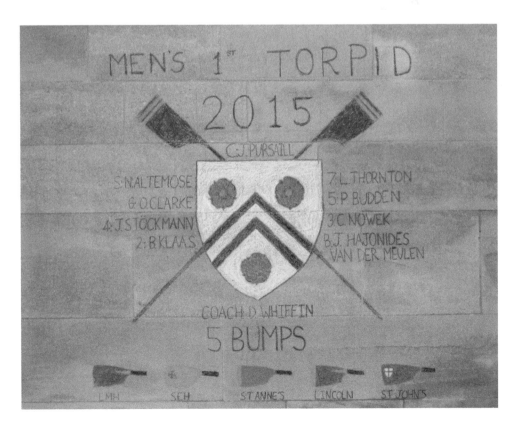

The gatehouse to Christ Church College was designed to form a grand entrance to Thomas Wolsey's Cardinal College. The domed bell tower that tops it was designed by Christopher Wren to house Great Tom, the former bell of Oseney Abbey, which each evening rang the curfew for the whole university.

the gate. At 6.00 a.m. on May Morning the High Street and Magdalen Bridge are thronged with crowds to witness another Oxford tradition – the college choir singing the *Hymnus Eucharisticus* from the top of Magdalen Tower.

'Oxford walls have a way of belittling us', i.e. they endure, we are mortal (quoted from Max Beerbohm, *Zuleika Dobson*). Many of those who studied there never, deep in their hearts, really leave. Every returning alumnus walks the pavements of their own memory – for them nothing has changed; their past is always both present and future. The magic of the place makes a lasting impression on many day visitors too, though perceived through a collective refracting lens: 'as it was in the beginning, is now and ever shall be'. Even Adolf Hitler coveted Oxford. He earmarked it as his capital once he had bombed London flat and invaded Britain, so it was spared the destruction of the Blitz despite being a prime candidate for the so-called Baedeker Raids (named after a series of German tourist guides). Reader, weave your own dreams!

There is much to see in Oxford, but this book does not take the visitor building by building, street by street on an 'architecture crawl'. Instead, it sets out to trace the history of both town and university, and to point the reader to the testimony of the surviving fragments. On the way, it tries to sketch the outlines of the origin and development of those two almost mythic protagonists, town and gown. So the reader is equipped to understand rather than simply to appreciate or notice.

An important note: colleges are not museums, but places in which communities of students and academics live and work. As a result, they are often closed to visitors in term time and particularly during the exam period. Most are open at advertised times, especially during the university vacations, though they may charge an entrance fee. Please respect the privacy of those who live there.

A busker in Cornmarket.

Looking up the High Street towards the spire of St Mary the Virgin. University College is on the left, while All Souls College is on the right beyond the row of seventeenth- and eighteenth-century shops. J. M. W. Turner painted the High Street from a similar viewpoint in 1810; the Ashmolean has recently acquired the picture.

2. A Town is Born

The origin of Oxford is blanketed in mist. Anthony Wood, the seventeenth-century antiquary, recites several foundation legends which were presumably current in his day: that Oxford was founded by Mempricius, King of the Britons, in BC 1009; or by Cassibulan, King of the Britons, around BC 58; or by Olenus Calenus, a Roman, *c.* 70 AD. The names are fictional and the dates far too early.

The first settlement worthy of the name in this now-favoured spot was certainly Saxon, though its fragmentary details are only now being teased from the earth. The location had the criterion of desirability. A promontory of well-drained gravel commands the confluence of the Rivers Thames and Cherwell, leaving any settlement protected on two sides and exposed only to the north. The rivers here were fordable, granting a strategic importance and attracting through trade.

Limited evidence of prehistoric activity – Neolithic, Bronze Age and Iron Age – has been found in the general area of Oxford. For example, a Beaker burial was excavated in St Thomas' Street together with possible evidence of ploughing, the ring ditches which encircle Bronze-Age burial mounds can be seen as cropmarks in aerial photographs of the University Parks, and part of an Iron-Age settlement in the Parks was examined. None of this represents a continuity of occupation and is better characterised as a series of short-term settlements or activities. In the Roman period the area to the east of Oxford extending southwards along the Thames valley developed into an industrial zone specialising in pottery manufacture. Many kiln sites have been excavated archaeologically, including a group on the site of the Churchill Hospital. However, the closest Roman towns were Dorchester and Abingdon. There was no Roman settlement on the site of modern Oxford.

The first written mention of Oxford is on a silver penny of King Alfred the Great (who died 899) where it is spelled *Ohsnaford*. Then the *Anglo-Saxon Chronicle* for 911–12 records, 'In this year died Æthelred, ealdorman of Mercia, and King Edward took over London and Oxford and all the lands which belonged thereto'. (Æthelred was ruler of Mercia and married to Edward's sister, Æthelflæd, Lady of the Mercians, so was son-in-law to Alfred.) Clearly a town of some note was already established by that date.

Evidence for an earlier origin is provided by the legend of St Frideswide who died in 727. Frideswide was the daughter of a minor Anglo-Saxon king named Didan. He founded a nunnery for her at Oxford, where she ruled as abbess over a house of twelve noble women. This would make it one of several religious sites in the Upper Thames founded by minor kings in the late seventh and early eighth centuries. Her legend goes on to say that despite having taken the veil, she was pursued by her suitor, a King Algar of Leicester, who planned to abduct and forcibly marry her. Versions vary but are agreed that he was miraculously struck blind allowing Frideswide to return to her nunnery. Tradition also allows for her to have sought safe haven in a wood at Binsey, just a short distance

The Cherwell, Oxford's other river, meets the Thames just beyond Christ Church Meadow.

north-west of Oxford. There she built a church, and a healing well (known as St Margaret's Well) appeared in response to her prayers. As an act of Christian charity, she restored the sight of the over-sexed Algar who had learned his lesson and meekly returned home. The well remained a site of pilgrimage and is still visited today. The lady herself became patron saint of both town and university. Her feast is celebrated on 19 October.

Exactly where was St Frideswide's convent, and what did early eighth-century Oxford look like? The consensus is that her nunnery was beneath Christ Church College, on the site of the present cathedral, though no identifiable traces have been found. That spot may have been chosen because it was close to a ford of the Thames and so would attract passing worshippers and their donations. If a small settlement already existed to service the needs of travellers, the planting of a religious house would only have increased its prosperity. Apart from a few sherds of pottery, little of this early settlement is known, but it must have been clustered around St Aldate's.

Oxford (*Oxenaford*) is prosaically interpreted to mean 'ford for oxen', and it was this which dictated the location of the first settlement and St Frideswide's convent. Remarkably, recent archaeological work has actually identified the ford (near the site of Folly Bridge). The river channel was quite shallow and braided, with a number of small islands of silt separated by watercourses, so the river could be crossed at most seasons by wading and island hopping. Astonishingly, a service trench beneath St Aldate's found an early Saxon stone surface, possibly a causeway which became a ford depending on the weather. Upright posts suggest that by the mid Saxon period a wooden

St Frideswide was venerated from the earliest times and her shrine became a place of pilgrimage. The shrine which can be seen today was probably erected in 1289. Following desecration at the Reformation, its fragments were reassembled by the Victorians. Medieval pilgrims left valuable gifts, so the watching chamber beside it allowed the canons to maintain security. (By kind permission of the Dean & Canons of Christ Church)

bridge with a surface around 3.3 m wide crossed at least part of the way. At one point hoofprints preserved in the mud confirm that oxen did indeed cross here! A late Saxon stone-surfaced ford 7 m wide was laid alongside the earlier bridge. At the same time, the townsfolk had begun the long-running battle to consolidate the river bank and to reclaim land by dumping waste behind timber revetments, gradually extending the riverfront.

The small settlement clustered around the gate of St Frideswide's foundation no doubt had its ups and downs until a momentous decision in the final years of the ninth century secured its future. King Alfred the Great of Wessex famously defeated the invading Danish Army at the Battle of Ethandun in 878 and made a favourable treaty with their king. No sooner was one threat nullified than another emerged: Vikings began raiding at will up the Thames. In order to defend the borders of Wessex, Alfred created a series of fortified places or *burhs*, most of which are still towns today. Along the upper Thames he fortified Wallingford, where his defences still survive, Oxford and Cricklade – though there is uncertainty as to whether this project was carried through by Alfred or his son Edward, later known as 'the Elder'. Oxford, on the frontier between the kingdoms of Wessex and Mercia, was probably chosen because it was a forward position on Mercian soil and commanded an important river crossing. At this time the town appears to have been laid out in a grid pattern and encircled with an earthen rampart 13 m wide. The presumably haphazard earlier settlement would have been swept away, making the new *burh*, in effect, a new foundation. The urban area was divided into plots and the main streets were surfaced – traces of their surfaces have been identified during roadworks, while some street frontages have barely altered over the intervening millennium. Alfred's layout still forms the skeleton of the modern town centre.

This new town was squarish in shape, extending roughly from St Michael's church on Cornmarket in the north to St Aldate's church in the south, and from St Mary the Virgin on the High Street in the east to Bullwarks Lane in the west. The road which was laid inside the rampart to allow troop movement survives in the modern street plan. In the east, Oriel Street and Schools Street may be on the line of this intramural road, while Catte Street and Magpie Lane mark the edge of the external ditch. The defensive circuit looped to the south to take in St Frideswide's priory with its minster church, and then followed the natural line of the terrace edge overlooking the floodplain. Within just a few years the *burh* was extended eastwards almost as far as Longwall Street, presumably to improve control of the crossing of the River Cherwell near what is today Magdalen Bridge. At the same time its rampart was faced in stone. The town was, presumably, thriving.

The oldest building in Oxford is the tower of St Michael's church on the corner of Cornmarket and Ship Street. Classic Saxon 'long-and-short' masonry can be seen at the corners, while the round-topped windows are divided by shaped balusters. However, its story is confusing. When the tower was first built in the first half of the eleventh century it was not attached to the nave of the church; rather, it was built into the town wall to form part of the north gate. A blocked doorway can be made out at street level, giving onto Cornmarket. This is difficult to explain liturgically, and one suggestion is that it provided pedestrian access through the base of the tower when the main town gates were closed. Another doorway, at second-floor level on the north side, may have opened onto the wall walk. Within only a short period, the rampart and ditch were diverted northwards a few meters to allow space for a church and graveyard, though the tower remained an integral part of the north gate throughout the Middle Ages.

Archaeological evidence for shops and houses within the town becomes plentiful from the late tenth century and they begin spread down towards the ford. The street frontages of the main thoroughfares were heavily built up, with the rear of plots used as gardens or for craft activities. The buildings were probably single storey, made of timber and perhaps infilled with cob (packed earth). Post holes, floors of compact clay or gravel and burnt daub are found in many excavations. The most notable features are cellars cut into the gravel, some just a few meters square and others full undercrofts. An early eleventh-century plank-lined example beneath All Saints' church in the High Street measured 3.5 x 6.5 m. The smaller cellars may have been for the storage of goods and valuables below shops or houses, while semi-subterranean undercrofts could be used by craftsmen as workshops and shops. Rubbish pits are common in the back plots.

Alfred's town was centred on the crossroads at Carfax, said to be derived from the French *Quatre Voies* meaning 'four ways' or *Carrefour* meaning 'crossroads', from which the four main streets radiated towards the cardinal points. The church of St Martin, founded before 1032, watched over this busy crossroads. The building was demolished in 1896 to allow for road widening, though visitors still climb its free-standing tower to enjoy the view. A church stood beside each of the main gateways through the rampart. St Michael at the Northgate has already been discussed. Another church of St Michael stood at the south gate. Initially St Mary the Virgin stood by the east gate, but when the *burh* was extended eastwards a new

Above: Cornmarket, St Aldate's and the bell tower of Christ Church College from St Michael's church.

Left: The Saxon tower of St Michael's church, Cornmarket, is the oldest building in Oxford, dating from the first half of the eleventh century. Note the characteristic 'long and short' work at its corners and the heavy balusters in the windows.

St Martin's tower in Carfax is all that remains of the church which was taken down in 1896. The tower is another favourite spot from which to view Oxford's rooftops. A pair of mechanical figures strike the quarter hours.

church of Holy Trinity was built to serve that purpose. Finally, the demolished church of St George in the Castle may have marked the original west gate.

Another early church is St Ebbe's, founded before 1005, although it was heavily restored in the nineteenth century. Its west doorway is early however, and its decoration of zig-zags and beaked heads suggests a date near 1170. It has been suggested that, together with St Aldate's and St Frideswide minster, it formed a line of three churches, which is an arrangement attested from Saxon monastic sites and may have been related to the needs of processions. Archaeological observations during reordering St Aldate's in 1999 recovered part of a tenth-century cross-shaft with knotwork decoration from the nave wall. Its original location is uncertain, but it is another piece of evidence for middle Saxon religious activity in the area. A sheela-na-gig, a rather explicit female fertility figure, is kept in the tower at St Michael's.

These were unstable times, but despite the political climate Oxford was a prosperous trading centre commanding a major east–west crossing point of the Thames at the frontier between the opposing states of Wessex and Mercia. Corn, wool, cloth and leather were economically important for the town in the Middle Ages and were surely established trades from the earliest periods. Excavation has produced hard evidence for a wide range of small-scale crafts: butchery, leather working, horn working, metal working and smithing, cloth production and flax retting. Off-cuts from shoe manufacture have been preserved in the river silts. There was a mint in the town from the late 890s. The spindle whorls and bone needles of industrious housewives are also found. It was not alone in attracting a resident population of Danish merchants to exploit the commercial opportunities on offer. King Æthelred II ('the Unready') became uneasy at the presence of so many aliens 'like cockle amongst the wheat', and in 1002 he issued a decree that all the Danes in his kingdom should be taken by surprise and slaughtered on St Brice's Day, 13 November. By chance we know what happened in Oxford. The Danish population fled to the minster church in St Frideswide's priory and barricaded themselves in, no doubt hoping to claim sanctuary. When the mob was unable to break in, it burned the church to the ground around them. The church was subsequently rebuilt.

Æthelred's fear may not have been entirely unfounded. Despite its defences, Oxford was sacked and burned by Swein's Danish Army in 1009 – the *Anglo-Saxon Chronicle* sounds overawed, calling it 'that immense hostile host'. They were back in 1010, and again in 1013 when the townsfolk surrendered and gave hostages as a guarantee of tribute and obedience.

Things to See

-St Michael's tower, Cornmarket, the oldest building in Oxford and a good point from which to view the rooftops.

-St Martin's tower, Carfax, another popular viewpoint. The original church and tower were Saxon, though the present tower is medieval.

-Within the cathedral, the existing shrine and watching chamber of St Frideswide are medieval, but mark a much earlier tradition of pilgrimage.

3. Before the University

Before the university emerged, Oxford was an ordinary town, indistinguishable from many across the South and Midlands. The Domesday Book of 1086 appears to record a town in decline: inside and outside the walls there were 1,018 properties of which almost 500 were waste or assessed as too poor to pay tax. We learn, for example, that the canons of St Frideswide's minster held fifteen properties in the town of which half were vacant. It is not clear whether this was a result of aggressive policies pursued by the new Norman rulers as they secured their land, or of longer-term economic stagnation. What these figures do show is that large areas within the walls remained undeveloped, as gardens, yards or empty plots.

Robert d'Oilly, one of William the Conqueror's followers, was entrusted with the security of Oxford. In 1071 he built a simple motte and bailey castle inside the west gate, in the process sweeping away a block of the Saxon town. The west gate appears to have been moved northwards at this time and the main road diverted around the new castle – a decision which is fossilised in the bend in Queen Street. D'Oilly's 65-ft-high earthen motte still commands the western approach to the core of the old town. His castle was upgraded over the centuries: at one time the motte was crowned with a shell keep of which no trace remains, while a well chamber deep within the mound provided insurance against a siege. The castle continued as an administrative centre, being converted into a gaol in the seventeenth century, and now reborn as a recreational area. The former church of St George in the Castle may have stood at the west gate before d'Oilly built his castle. Although d'Oilly's church has gone, its crypt survives. The prominent St George's Tower may have served as a detached bell tower, doubling as a defensive structure (similar to St Michael at the Northgate).

Robert d'Oilly's great benefaction to the town was the building of Grandpont (a forerunner of Folly Bridge). This was a stone causeway perhaps 700 m long on the line of the ancient ford, making access to and through the town reliable at all seasons. In this way he confirmed, for centuries to come, its economic position as the premier crossing point on this section of the river. Roadworks occasionally uncover the stonework of his causeway encased in the modern roadway. An unexpected benefit of this project was an increase in silting, which led to land reclamation beside the river. An early bridge over the Cherwell on the site of the modern Magdalen Bridge was, by analogy, known as Pettypont.

Already by the time of the Domesday Book houses were beginning to creep outside the walls. Soon suburbs began to develop. Tenements were spreading down St Aldate's towards the bridge, built on reclaimed land prone to flooding; some plots were so poorly drained that they remained as gardens until the seventeenth century. Suburban growth outside the west gate began earlier. An Augustinian priory (later abbey) was founded in 1129 by Robert d'Oilly the younger on the low-lying isle of Oseney just a short distance

The 64-ft-high earthen mound (or motte) of Robert d'Oilly's castle, built in 1071, would originally have been topped with a wooden defensive tower.

A 54-ft-deep well beneath the castle mound is accessed via this steep staircase.

St George's Tower (right) stood on the curtain wall of the medieval castle, though it may have doubled as the bell tower for the chapel of St George in the castle. The castle became a gaol in the seventeenth century, though the present buildings date from around 1800.

outside the town wall. Its endowment included some neighbouring land which the priory immediately began to develop in order to gain rents. The priory built the church of St Thomas the Martyr (initially dedicated to St Nicholas) to serve the spiritual needs of the new community. This church was heavily restored in the nineteenth century, making it difficult to see what of the original building survives. This was a poor suburb, and environmental evidence from excavations paints a picture of 'filth and decay', with beetles eating the timbers and living in the thatch, and piles of rotting refuse and dung. In contrast, the abbey became wealthy. When the monasteries were dissolved, its abbot was appointed as the first bishop of the new Oxford diocese with its huge abbey church 100 yards long serving briefly as his cathedral before that honour was transferred to St Frideswide's. From that date the ruins were quarried for building materials. Agas's map of 1578 shows the abbey as derelict, though some of the buildings survived into the nineteenth century. All that remains today of the great Oseney Abbey is a small fifteenth-century building (in private ownership).

To the north, St Giles was built up in the late twelfth/early thirteenth centuries. The church of St Giles itself, wedged into the junction of the Woodstock and Banbury Roads, was first mentioned in 1138, presumably recently built to serve a growing extra-mural community. It has been extensively adapted and restored over the centuries, but a few fragments including the base of the tower and the arched clerestory windows on the north side may be original. The manor of Holywell was a separate manor at the time of Domesday, while its parish church of St Cross was built around 1160 – the chancel arch is of that date. The church and manor house still give a village air to the corner of Manor Road.

Left: The church of St Thomas in Becket Street was founded in 1141 by Oseney Abbey to serve the newly created suburb outside the west gate. Despite Victorian restoration, this priest's door, with the remains of a sundial above, is thirteenth century.

Below: This nondescript structure is the sole remaining building of the once-great Oseney Abbey.

St Giles' was the parish church for the northern suburb. It is first mentioned in the early twelfth century, but much of the present building dates from 100 years later.

By the twelfth century the town was growing prosperous. Economic life thrived. Two weekly markets in the High Street overflowed down the side streets. Merchants dealing in particular goods tended to cluster together; for example the top of the High Street was a shambles, known as Butchers' Strete, St Aldate's became known as Fish Street and Northgate Street became Cornmarket. Other quarters were known for their vintners, mercers, cutlers and even goldsmiths. References are increasingly made to stone houses, presumably occupied by the leading burgesses or local landowners. Frewin Hall was one such house, occupying a ½ ha plot between Cornmarket and New Inn Hall Street. Built in the earlier twelfth century, it was owned by Geoffrey fitzDurand, a wealthy burgess. In 1435 it passed to St Mary's College, but was demolished following the Dissolution of the Monasteries under Henry VIII. A grand half-timbered house now occupies the site, though the original vaulted undercroft measuring 14.5 x 5 m survives as a cellar.

In common with many towns, Oxford was home to a small Jewish population. A few were wealthy merchants and money lenders: Walter of Merton bought a tenement from Jacob, son of Moses, as part of the foundation plot for Merton College. Most were poor, and yet they were disproportionately the victims of periodic persecution. When, in 1268, all Oxford was outraged at a surely concocted tale of damage to a processional cross, the whole Jewish community was fined for complicity and the funds used to erect a marble cross outside St John's church. Then in 1290 all Jews were expelled from England. Little evidence of their sojourn in Oxford remains. A plaque in Blue Boar Street commemorates

Many timber-framed buildings survive around the city, though most are faced with plaster. This good example stands on the corner of Cornmarket and Ship Street, seen here from the churchyard of St Michael's.

the Great Jewry and the site of their synagogue is now beneath Tom Quad, Christ Church College. The former Jewish cemetery is marked by a plaque in the Botanic Gardens; the path named Deadman's Walk which runs behind Merton was reputedly the route for their funeral processions.

Medieval Oxford was a town rich in churches. St Frideswide, the mother church of the town, was refounded as a priory of regular Augustinian canons around 1120. Many of the other churches or chapels had pre-Conquest origins, even if they were largely rebuilt and enlarged during the Middle Ages. St Aldate's (the name of this unknown saint is possibly a corruption of Old Gate, reflecting its antiquity), St Ebbe's and St Mary the Virgin have been mentioned previously, as have the four gate churches of St Michael at the Northgate, St Michael at the Southgate, Holy Trinity at the Eastgate and possibly also St George in the Castle. The crypt of St Peter-in-the-East (now the library of St Edmund Hall and closed to visitors) dates from 1130–40. While the standing masonry is Norman and medieval, traces of an earlier stone and timber church take its origins back to the tenth century. All Saints', now the library of Lincoln College (also closed), was founded in the late eleventh century. The Saxon St Martin's defined the heart of the town, and other medieval churches were St Edward the Martyr, St Mildred and St Peter-le-Bailey. The church of St John the Baptist is first mentioned in 1206, becoming Merton College chapel after 1292. Outside the gates to the west were St Budoc, which became the chapel of the Friars of the Sack in 1265, and St Thomas the Martyr founded by Oseney abbey. St Mary Magdalen and St Giles served the suburb outside the north gate, while St Clement served the community across Magdalen Bridge (its site marked by a stone on The Plain roundabout; the present church is entirely of 1828).

Although Oxford was in many ways an ordinary market town, it began to attract royal patronage. Henry I had a favoured hunting lodge at Woodstock, and Oxford was a convenient stopping point on the journey from London. In around 1130 he built Beaumont Palace outside the north gate beside what is now Beaumont Street. By 1133 this 'new hall' was sufficiently comfortable for the royal court to celebrate Easter there, when thanks were offered for the safe birth of the future Henry II. It continued to be popular with royalty: Richard the Lionheart and his brother John were both born here. The royal connection continued, with parliament occasionally held at the palace. Gradually its function became increasingly administrative rather than residential, until at least part of the complex was leased out. At the disastrous Battle of Bannockburn in 1314, Edward II vowed to found a Carmelite friary if he escaped with his life, and in fulfilment he gave the now out-of-favour Beaumont Palace to the order. Following the Dissolution of the Monasteries the buildings went into a slow decline as they were robbed for building materials. A drawing of 1785 shows some masonry still standing within a derelict site.

Oxford was destined to play a large and costly part in the civil war known as The Anarchy. When Henry I died he left a daughter, the Empress Matilda (known as Empress because she had married the Holy Roman Emperor Henry V, though by this date he had died). This triggered a succession crisis as the barons were not ready for a queen, so Henry's nephew Stephen of Blois seized the crown. The early years of his reign were marked by unrest, and in 1139 Matilda landed in England intent on reclaiming her throne with the help of Robert of Gloucester, her half-brother. Robert d'Oilly the younger was one of those who declared for her, and was able to bring a strong castle to the cause. The campaign quickly reached a stalemate, until in 1142 Stephen trapped Matilda in Oxford Castle. One snowy night just before Christmas she slipped quietly away across the frozen river, supposedly wearing a white cloak for camouflage, and took refuge in Wallingford Castle before moving on to Devizes. Stephen's frustrated forces ravaged and burned Oxford, which still presumably cowered behind its Saxon rampart. The conflict wore on inconclusively until 1153 when Stephen's son Eustace died. There seemed little left to fight for, so peace was concluded and Stephen recognised Matilda's son Henry (later Henry II) as his heir. With this renewed stability, the town's prosperity seems to have bounced back quickly.

The ninth-century town rampart was rebuilt in masonry in the thirteenth century, almost precisely on the same line. The best surviving portions may be seen in the gardens of New College and Merton. A ditch outside the walls formed a dry moat. Apart from the four main gates, further small posterns were granted for local convenience, some for the use of monasteries or colleges whose land crossed the wall. However, this defence was not to be tested until the mid seventeenth century, by which time it was woefully out of date. For the civic authorities, its roles as a status symbol, a barrier to reduce tax avoidance and a protection from vagabonds were more important.

Health, as well as violence, meant life in the Middle Ages was precarious. Despite the teaching of medicine at the university, effective treatments were few and the ineffective ones were expensive. One feared illness was leprosy, a term which covered a variety of

New College (founded 1379) was built into an angle of the town defences, with part of its perimeter defined by the town wall. Today, the best preserved portion of the wall can be seen in the college gardens. (With permission)

skin diseases. Leper hospitals were endowed by the wealthy as acts of charity, although their function was to house rather than treat sufferers. Oxford was served by the leper hospital of St Bartholomew (also known as St Bartlemas), which was founded by Henry I for twelve lepers (known by the monastic term 'brethren') and a chaplain who was warden. It was safely isolated a mile outside the town in Cowley Marsh. Edward III presented the hospital with a valuable relic, the skin of its patron saint, Bartholomew the apostle (who was martyred by being flayed alive). After two centuries of mismanagement the hospital was transferred in 1329 to the newly founded Oriel College, which rebuilt the timber chapel in stone. When leprosy ceased to be a scourge in England, its buildings were adapted as a retreat for college members in time of plague. Today its chapel survives as a small and secluded fragment of medieval England tucked away (down a private lane) behind the busy Cowley Road.

Another twelfth-century foundation, the Hospital of St John, stood immediately outside the east gate. The hospital was surrendered to Bishop Waynflete to make way for his foundation of Magdalen College in the later fifteenth century. A blocked doorway on Magdalen's High Street frontage was the entrance to the former Hospital. Along with the buildings of the suppressed hospital, Magdalen College took over the tradition of preaching a public open-air sermon on St John the Baptist's Day (24 June). The stone pulpit in St John's Quad was built for this purpose; the tradition lapsed but was revived in 1896, weather permitting.

The chapel of the former St Bartholomew's leper hospital, tucked away down a private road behind Cowley Road.

A blocked gateway in the High Street frontage of Magdalen College is all that remains of the twelfth-century Hospital of St John, which was surrendered to make way for the college.

Among other token provisions for the disabled and frail elderly were the almshouses established by Cardinal Wolsey in St Aldate's directly opposite his new college. This two-storey cottage-like building was purchased by Pembroke in 1888 for its own use as accommodation.

Access to clean water was a perennial problem in all towns. Even this watery location at the confluence of two rivers was no exception. Archaeologists frequently find wells in the open areas behind the street frontages – simple pits dug through the gravel to the water table – though these same areas were also filled with pits for disposing of rubbish and 'waste'. Oxford found a civic benefactor in the lawyer Otho Nicholson who brought clean water from a spring on Hinksey Hill to the west of the town to a new public fountain in Carfax. The Conduit (fountain) operated from around 1617 until 1787 when it was found to be in the way of street improvements. It was bought by Lord Harcourt and re-erected on his estate at nearby Nuneham Courtenay to serve as an ornamental feature. Although the Conduit is on private land, the small Conduit House at North Hinksey may be visited.

Things to See

-Tours of the castle are available, and the motte is a good vantage point. Do not fail to visit the well chamber deep within the mound.

-A plaque in Blue Boar Street commemorates the Great Jewry.

-A plaque beside the entrance to the Botanic Gardens commemorates the Jewish cemetery.

-The blocked gateway on Magdalen's High Street frontage is all that can be seen of the twelfth-century hospital of St John.

-The open-air pulpit in Magdalen College.

The former almshouses founded by Cardinal Wolsey opposite Christ Church (Cardinal) College on St Aldate's. The range now provides accommodation for Pembroke College.

The seventeenth-century Conduit House at North Hinksey, from which fresh water was channelled to the public conduit in Carfax. (In the care of English Heritage)

4. A University Emerges

The familiar coat of arms which appears on Oxford University Press books had official sanction by 1429. It shows an open book with seven seals, and the motto *dominus illuminatio mea* between three gold crowns on a blue field. The book represents learning; the motto translates as 'enlightened by the Lord'; the seals probably refer to the seven mystical seals of the book of Revelation; while the crowns perpetuate the legend that the university was founded by Saxon kings, and particularly by the most famous of them all, Alfred the Great.

Today the name 'Oxford' is synonymous worldwide with 'university'. That was not always the case. The origins of study and higher education in Oxford are very shadowy. In the twelfth century grammar schools sprang up in many English towns to teach literacy – which meant Latin – to meet the growing administrative needs of the church, state and great landowners. Oxford was no different, and the first schoolmaster there, Theobald of Etampes, is recorded in 1095–1125. But this was not a university! English students seeking a higher education in theology, canon or civil law, or medicine would go to the established universities of Europe, of which Paris and Bologna were the foremost.

A masters degree was required in order to teach the higher disciplines. These 'masters' were essentially freelance teachers independent of any institution – wandering scholars looking for a suitable place in which to earn their livelihoods. The most promising conditions were provided by a town with a large clerical and legal presence. That meant somewhere in which ecclesiastical or civil courts met regularly. In such places prospective students might be recruited in sufficient numbers. In the middle decades of the twelfth century Northampton satisfied these conditions and began to attract masters and students, forming the nucleus of a 'proto-university', but its influence declined. By contrast, Oxford on its strategic river crossing was increasingly recognised as a centre of communications. The rapidly growing ecclesiastical courts found the town a convenient location to meet, drawing around them a community of clerics and lawyers. The newly founded Augustinian priory at Oseney, just outside the walls, and the colleges of priests at St Frideswide's minster and St George in the Castle, added to their numbers. Important ecclesiastical councils were held in the town. Perhaps due to the presence of the royal palace, the town also developed as a centre for government. These were exactly the conditions the masters were on the lookout for.

There is no foundation date for the university in Oxford for the very good reason that it was not founded but gradually emerged. It was created by dozens of independent decisions by independent masters, not as a central plan. The names of these pioneers are not known but by the final decades of the twelfth century Oxford was beginning to establish a tentative reputation as a place of higher study for those who did not wish or could not afford to go to the continental universities. It would have taken little at this point for Oxford to go the way of Northampton. Then in the 1190s war with France made study abroad difficult, if not impossible, and masters and students alike sought personal safety at home. They looked for suitable places to continue their studies, and the rising reputation of Oxford acted as a magnet. In the two decades between 1190 and 1209 it is likely there were at least seventy masters at Oxford, possibly more, in particular teaching theology and the liberal arts. The number of students at any one time is difficult to estimate, but was certainly several hundreds (perhaps 2,000 by 1310). These students were all technically 'in holy orders', that is, they were on the lowest rungs of the Church's hierarchy which made them subject to religious rather than civic discipline. Chapel attendance continued to be a requirement on students well into the twentieth century.

The independent masters found it expedient to work together for practical purposes and came together to form a craft guild – the university grew out of such a guild. Even at this early date there were tensions between the town and the cuckoo in its nest. This is unsurprising, as the townsfolk had to cope with a large influx of youths who were full of spirit but short of money. From the opposite perspective, this academic body was a captive market ripe for exploiting. As always, fair rents were a point of friction. So the masters formed a committee to negotiate with the town burgesses over rents: this was the first example of the masters acting as a body. Then in 1201 a papal letter named one John Grim as *magister scholarum Oxoniae* (head of the scholars of Oxford). It would be a mistake to accept this as evidence that one man governed all the masters, still less that Oxford University had become a formal institution; he was more probably first among equals for certain restricted purposes. For example, if the masters were to agree on standards of discipline or on academic standards for granting degrees, their guild needed a convenor and chairman.

Town and gown is an enduring divide. While the fledgling university found ways to flex its limited muscle in dealings with the civic administration, some students found the temptations all around them too great. This fuelled town-gown tensions, which occasionally spilled over into rioting and violence. One noteworthy occasion was in 1209. When a student killed his mistress and fled, the town authorities responded by hanging two other students. This was going too far, infringing their rights as clerics, and the masters agreed to suspend all teaching in protest. This was not just an empty gesture but a very real economic sanction against the town as the academic body mostly left, taking their purchasing power with them. Some found a permanent new home at Cambridge. It fell to the papal legate to find a resolution to this stand-off, and his final settlement was a triumph for the masters and humiliation for the town. The town was to pay 52s annually for the use of poor scholars and was to provide a free dinner for 100 every St Nicholas's Day, rents were pegged and a the price of food regulated, and any clerk (i.e. student or master) arrested by the town was to be handed over to the bishop of Lincoln's officer effectively removing him from civic jurisdiction. All this was set out in a charter which was binding in perpetuity. The solid authority behind this decision rested with the bishop, who was to appoint a deputy or 'chancellor' to oversee the scholars. This provision was a clear sign of the corporate recognition of the academic body by those in authority.

The most significant of all town-gown riots took place on St Scholastica's Day (10 February) 1355. It allegedly began in the Swyndlestock Tavern on the corner of Queen

A modern statue in the churchyard of St Peter-in-the-East, now the library of St Edmund Hall, represents St Edmund of Abingdon. St Edmund (d. 1240) was a university teacher who later became Archbishop of Canterbury.

Street and St Aldate's when insults were traded over the quality of the beer. In no time all the town's pent up frustration against the privileges of the university boiled over into indiscriminate violence. The official investigation was swift to lay the blame, and hence the punishment, squarely on the town. The charter issued in June of that year was to define the relationship between the two bodies for the next half millennium. By it, the chancellor acquired a number of valuable rights, including the right to check the quality and price of bread, ale and wine and the weights used by merchants – even the right to enforce street cleaning. The university firmly gained the upper hand and town authorities lost out heavily.

As an association of masters with little institutional structure, the university owned little property – it did not need to. It offered few central facilities. It was not concerned with the accommodation of students, which was left to the initiative of individual masters, though it did regulate the academic halls they lodged in as well as rents and prices in the town. Important documents and cash were secured in a chest in St Mary's church: the finance department is still called the University Chest. The lecture rooms (or 'schools') it needed were mostly rented, for example in 1440 Oseney Abbey speculatively erected a two-storey range of arts schools in School Street to lease to the university.

The corporate body which was the university only came together when the regent masters (MAs with university, or later college, posts) were summoned in Congregation to transact business – as they still do. At first, these business meetings probably took place in St Mary the Virgin. Then, in the 1320s, a purpose-built two-storey structure known as the Congregation House was added onto the north side of the church. It was the first building owned by the university. The Congregation met on the ground floor, and the first floor housed the university's small library, bequeathed by Bishop Cobham. These precious books were, of course, all in manuscript and were reserved for the use of senior members of the university. Undergraduate teaching depended on lectures and oral exercises rather than access to books, though significant passages could be copied by hand. When the library was later moved, meetings of the Congregation relocated to the better lit room upstairs.

The undergraduate curriculum of the medieval university concentrated on the Arts (hence BA and MA) – grammar, logic and rhetoric, known as the *trivium*, and arithmetic, geometry, music and astronomy, known as the *quadrivium*, together forming the seven liberal arts. The goal was to learn to dispute well. It was assumed a student already had Latin, the language of study and of everyday life. University statutes specified at least seven years of study between matriculating (entering the university as an undergraduate) and receiving a masters degree. (This is still true today: after graduating BA a former student must wait four years before paying £25

Today the vaulted lower room of the former Congregation House has been repurposed as the church's café.

to be admitted MA.) After that, a number of courses of study were open to him in the 'higher faculties' of theology, law – canon and civil – and medicine, the pinnacle being a doctorate in theology. The friars were to cause conflict when they tried to enrol in the faculty of Theology without first becoming Masters of Arts. But this curriculum was not static. 'Humanism' or the 'new learning' introduced the Biblical languages of Greek and Hebrew to scholars in the West: previously the Scriptures, and even the classical authors such Aristotle, had been studied through Latin translations. By the start of the sixteenth century these languages were finding a place at Oxford, so that Regis professorships in both were established in 1540.

The university embarked on a new building venture in the 1420s. Theology was regarded as the highest form of study, so it was decided to build a Divinity School. It was to be one large lecture room measuring 87 ft x 31 ft. Possible patrons, including bishops and monastic houses, were approached for donations, but progress was slow. In 1439 a new master mason, Thomas Elkyn, was appointed in an attempt to push the work forwards. As an economy measure, he was instructed to build in a plainer style than that which his predecessor had used, eliminating 'frivolous curiosities'. Then, in 1444, Duke Humfrey of Gloucester, youngest son of Henry IV, made the university a gift of 281 volumes. This was so generous that the university undertook to build a new room to house it. This was to be a second storey over the as-yet-incomplete Divinity School. As a result of financial difficulties, the building was only finally completed in 1490. The old university library was moved to the new Duke Humfrey's Library, though access to this valuable resource was still limited to senior members. At the Reformation the library was broken up. During the visitation of Oxford University under Edward VI, the library was closely examined for heresy and most of its volumes apparently either burned or sold. This was so thorough that in 1555 it was decided to sell off the now redundant desks and hand the room over to the faculty of medicine.

In the more stable political climate of Elizabeth's reign, Sir Thomas Bodley's offer to restore the library at his own expense was gratefully accepted. When the refitted and restocked library was formally opened on 8 November 1602 security was paramount – some books were chained to their shelves while others were locked away for safety. Importantly, he provided an endowment to fund the management and growth of the collection. The attitude to learning and books was changing. It soon became apparent that the single chamber of Duke Humfrey's was not large enough to house the growing stock, so Bodley paid for an extension known as the Arts End. Today the university library is named the Bodleian Library in memory of its founding benefactor, and thanks to his negotiations with the Stationer's Company it is one of five copyright libraries in Britain which are entitled to receive a copy of every book published. He also initiated a project (which he could not fund himself but for which he could provide the driving enthusiasm) to replace the old and inadequate schools. The Schools Quadrangle, which forms three sides of a court in front of Bodley's library and the Divinity School, was completed in 1624. It represents the traditional curriculum set in stone, with the name of each 'school' or lecture room painted over the relevant doorway.

Above: The Bodleian Library, the main university library, first opened in 1602 due to the generosity and energy of Sir Thomas Bodley. The entrance from Schools Quad is seen here.

Right: A wall monument to Sir Thomas Bodley (d. 1613), the major benefactor who refounded the university's library, can be seen in Merton College chapel. Bodley is appropriately shown between piles of books. (With the permission of the Warden and Fellows of Merton College Oxford)

A doorway in Schools Quad, in front of the Bodleian. The painted wording announces the Faculties of Languages and of Geometry and Arithmetic.

Things to See

-Congregation House in St Mary the Virgin, High Street. The vaulted ground-floor room is now a café.

-An inscription on the wall of the Santander Bank in St Aldate's marking the site of the Swyndlestock Tavern, epicentre of the St Scholastica's Day riot.

-The fifteenth-century Divinity School, entered through the foyer of the Bodleian.

-The seventeenth-century Schools Quad, in front of the Bodleian Library, purpose-built as the teaching core of the university. The names of the faculties are still painted over their doors.

-In Merton College chapel, a wall-mounted memorial to Thomas Bodley appropriately shows him between stacks of books.

5. Halls, Monasteries and Colleges

The popular perception of Oxford revolves around its colleges, particularly the huddle of venerable buildings in the city centre, some self-effacing, others bursting with self-confidence. However, colleges were relative latecomers to the university.

Before the college system evolved, most students lived in one of the academic halls. These could be very basic. Each was under the control of a master who leased the building, and it closed if it was not economically viable. Life in a hall provided students with lodging, meals and much of their teaching. There were over a hundred such halls at the start of the fourteenth century, after which their numbers declined, largely as a result of amalgamations. They could be anything from a small house to purpose-built accommodation, and most would have been indistinguishable from their non-academic neighbours. As the university gained in corporate strength, it exercised increasing control over both discipline and academic life. Halls and their masters were registered annually by the Chancellor to maintain standards. Other, poorer students rented shared rooms from townsfolk and managed as best they could. In *The Miller's Tale*, written around 1386, Geoffrey Chaucer introduces Nicholas, a randy Oxford student who lodged with an elderly carpenter. Nicholas owned a set of astronomy textbooks, an astrolabe and a harp, but such possessions were expensive and certainly not typical.

Some buildings were converted, others purpose-built. Tackley's Inn in the High Street was built around 1300 by Roger le Mareschal, rector of Tackley, to be let out as an academic hall. It combined a row of single-storey shops on the street frontage with a hall and chambers behind. Part of the cellar and hall, together with a fifteenth-century roof, survive. Another purpose-built hall was White Hall, also in the High Street, by Bartholomew Bishop in 1381. It was better appointed than Tackley's, with a hall, buttery kitchen and chambers around three sides of a courtyard – halls were beginning to look a little like college quadrangles. As an alternative strategy, the neighbouring St Mary and Bedel Halls were amalgamated after 1451 to make economies of scale.

The hall system was gradually superseded. Only three continued into the modern era: in 1881 St Alban Hall was absorbed into neighbouring Merton College after years of close association; St Mary Hall was united with Oriel College in 1902. The only true survivor is St Edmund Hall (affectionately known as Teddy Hall), which has remained independent and was only accorded the status of a college in 1957.

Monasteries had always trained their novices, and personal theological study was an expectation of most orders. For example, the Benedictine *Rule* enjoins several hours of personal reading and study a day. As the university began to gain a reputation in the higher studies, it was natural that the religious orders should wish to benefit. It was obviously inappropriate for monks to lodge in halls or rooms in the town where they would be exposed to the temptations of the world and would find the pattern of daily

These façades in the High Street hide the remains of Tackley's Inn, a purpose-built academic hall dating from around 1300.

A corner of Front Quad, St Edmund Hall. The cottage-like accommodation on the left is *c.* 1596, while the more elaborate but unecclesiastical-looking chapel to the right dates from around 1680.

worship difficult to observe. The solution was for each order to establish its own *studium* or centre of academic study to which its houses across the country could confidently send their brightest.

The two preaching orders of friars, the Dominicans and Franciscans, were first to be drawn to the town, in 1221 and 1224, respectively. For them, learning had a practical application – to equip a brother to preach for the salvation of souls. Paradise Square occupies the site of the Franciscan 'paradise' or cloister garden. Little remains above ground. These orders were quickly followed by other friars: the Carmelites (1256–before Edward II's grant of the old Beaumont Palace), Austin friars (1266–67) and Friars of the Sack (1261–62). These new religious houses formed a ring outside the walls where sufficiently large plots could be acquired. The Franciscans' convent actually straddled the town wall, its church plugging the gap which had been created in the defences.

If the friars were early adopters, the monastic orders were slower to see the benefits of a university education. In 1281 the Cistercians established Rewley Abbey as their Oxford *studium*, though its role declined: in the nineteenth century its site was redeveloped for the LNWR station and is now occupied by the Said Business School. All that remains is a short section of fifteenth-century wall pierced by a doorway. The Cistercian college of St Bernard was initiated in 1437 though it was slow to develop. The Benedictines appear to have been altogether more committed to the education of their brethren. Gloucester College, opened in 1283, was designed to serve the whole order. Fifteen houses maintained lodgings there while at least forty houses sent students intermittently. The wealthy houses of Durham (1286), and after a pause Christ Church Canterbury (1361), established their own *studia*. A remarkable survival gives an idea of how one of these colleges may have been ordered. Over the centuries following its dissolution, Gloucester College morphed into Worcester College. The main quad contains a range of two-storey fifteenth-century buildings (or *camerae*) which look like cottages. They were the lodgings maintained by individual abbeys for their own students – a series of independent units within the larger whole. The coats of arms over the doorways identify the parent house: Glastonbury, Malmesbury, St Augustine Canterbury, Pershore. Part of the monastic kitchen also survives, a reminder of the brothers' communal life. In contrast, the Augustinian canons of Oseney and St Frideswide's appear not to have engaged with academic learning although they did let property to scholars on a commercial basis.

The concept of the college, which is today the defining feature of the townscape, was a late addition and developed alongside the older institution of the academic hall. Unlike the halls, colleges were self-governing corporate bodies, bound by statutes. Although these new colleges were intended as centres for academic study, a major duty was to pray for the souls of the founder and his family. The relationship of college and university, of one corporate body with another, mutually dependent yet proudly independent with their own constitutions and rights, has always been a source of tension. An uncomfortable 'federal' solution gradually developed.

The first college was Merton, founded in 1264 by Walter de Merton, lately chancellor to Henry III, who ended his career as bishop of Rochester (d. 1277). A 1-acre plot was assembled in St John's Lane from a number of small tenements, together with the neighbouring St John's church which served the scholars as a chapel. Mob Quad is often

A disused gateway through a stretch of old wall is the final remaining fragment of the Cistercian monastery of Rewley Abbey.

This range of cottages in the main court of Worcester College are the original accommodation of the monastic Gloucester College. Each housed student monks from a different Benedictine monastery, identified by their coats of arms over the doorways.

called the first quadrangle in Oxford, with gatehouse, hall for dining and lectures, and accommodation; unlike a monastery it had no cloister). The scrolled iron strap-work of the hall door is an original fitting of *c.* 1275. By 1291 a college chapel had been built and the church of St John was dismantled for its building materials. Being the first, Merton's layout and statutes became the models which other colleges adopted or reacted against.

University College followed in 1280 and Balliol in 1282. Then during the fourteenth century, Exeter (1314), Oriel (1326), The Queen's (1340) and New College (1379) were all founded. However, success was not guaranteed. Bishop Robert Burnell's attempt foundered due to his early death in 1292 before he had managed to build up an adequate endowment. Winwick College (1359–60) was another dream which failed due to the untimely death of its would-be founder.

Until this point these medieval colleges differed from the modern idea of a college in one very significant particular: they were all founded exclusively for graduates studying for higher degrees. Undergraduates still lived in the academic halls or in lodgings around the town. Of the traditional colleges, only All Souls has managed to retain its graduate-only status – although the concept of the graduate college was reincarnated in the later twentieth century to cope with changing patterns of study.

The age of the undergraduate college was born with the foundation of New College by William of Wykeham, bishop of Winchester, in 1379. He also founded Winchester College, a grammar school, and conceived his two colleges as part of a single educational scheme. Scholars (i.e. undergraduates) at New College were to have spent at least one year at Winchester College and be aged between fifteen and twenty. Wykeham's idea

Merton College's Mob Quad was the first quadrangle in Oxford and set the format for later colleges to follow. (With the permission of the Warden and Fellows of Merton College Oxford)

Above: The fourteenth-century Great Quad of New College, around which chapel, hall, library and accommodation were grouped. (With permission)

Left: Unlike Merton, New College (founded 1379) was given a traditional cloister as a place for meditation and study. The cloister is glimpsed here from Great Quad. (With permission)

of undergraduates in colleges was only slowly taken up, but as a statute of around 1410 required students to live either in halls or in colleges in order to combat perennial issues of discipline, the option was clearly recognised.

College foundation continued, with Lincoln (1427), All Souls (1438), Magdalen (1458), Brasenose (1509) and Corpus Christi (1517). Each community is a little different, as the founder's own idea of what their college should be was enshrined in its statutes. Magdalen's founder was another bishop of Winchester, William of Waynflete, who followed his predecessor's example by establishing Magdalen College School to allow his scholars to pass between the institutions.

Then came Cardinal Wolsey's ambitious but ultimately unwise plan to create the largest and most splendid college of all and name it Cardinal College in his own honour. Thomas Cromwell, later Chancellor of England, wrote to Wolsey in April 1528: 'Every man thinks the like was never seen for largeness, beauty, sumptuous, curious and substantial building' – surely intended as a warning rather than as praise! Wolsey's unprecedented wealth and power allowed him to take over the site of St Frideswide's priory, augmenting it with neighbouring properties, and suppressing several monasteries elsewhere to provide a lavish endowment. Work began in January 1525, but stopped dead at his fall from power in 1529. By this date the hall and kitchen were complete, two ranges of accommodation and the south-west tower were inhabitable, the gate tower was partially erected and the walls of the new chapel had reached head height – redundant, they were only demolished in the 1660s. The motif of a cardinal's cap still forlornly decorates the south-west tower. At Wolsey's fall, Henry VIII took over this project along with his other properties such as Hampton Court Palace. The college was briefly renamed King Henry VIII College and camped within its building site.

The sixteenth century was a time of chaos and reversals. Starting as an undoubtedly Catholic country, England ended the century as securely Protestant one, but the journey was not easy. The Dissolution of the Monasteries in the late 1530s, followed by the dissolution of the chantries a few years later, was a game-changer for Oxford. The extensive sites of the former monasteries ringed around the town became vacant while the monastic colleges within the walls were left without scholars or purpose – Canterbury, Durham, Gloucester, St Bernard's, and the Augustinian St Mary's. It was for a while uncertain whether the secular (non-monastic) colleges would share their fate and their endowments would be appropriated by the Crown, but a distinction was drawn. As the Reformation progressed, the requirement for scholars and fellows to be in holy orders ceased to be relevant.

Henry VIII College gained a new purpose when the cathedral was moved from the former Oseney Abbey to the old minster church of St Frideswide adjoining the college. It became – and remains – the college chapel and its dean and chapter were to be fellows of the college. The college was refounded as Christ Church (known to its members as The House), and its site was augmented with the addition of the former Benedictine Canterbury College providing a ready-made quad and facilities. Vacant monastic property was plentiful and presumably relatively cheap. In 1555 London merchant Sir Thomas White acquired St Bernard's College for his new foundation of St John's. The front quad is still largely the recycled monastic building. An almost identical future awaited the

Left: The Great Tower of Magdalen College was built as a bell tower around 1500 and is 144 feet high. By tradition, early on May Morning the college choir sings from the top.

Below: A decorative motif of cardinal's caps on the south-west tower of Christ Church College are a reminder of Wolsey's over-ambition and fall from power.

Right: Looking through the main gate of Christ Church College into Tom Quad, the largest quad in Oxford.

Below: The forbidding Victorian façade of the Meadow Buildings at Christ Church College which overlook Christ Church Meadow. Tourist access to the cathedral is through the central gateway.

former Durham College, which was purchased in 1555 by Sir Thomas Pope, a civil servant, to found Trinity College. Here Durham Quad perpetuates the old name, and its eastern range still dates from the early fifteenth century. In 1560 Gloucester Hall was founded, taking over the dilapidated buildings of the former Gloucester College. It was refounded in 1714 as Worcester College by Sir Thomas Cookes, a Worcestershire landowner, and despite its chequered history still preserves important monastic architecture. St Mary's College, New Inn Hall Street, was acquired by a townsman and demolished.

While Henry VIII was essentially conservative in religion, his young son, Edward VI, was of a more radical persuasion. Under Edward, many older fellows were ejected to be replaced with supporters of the new faith, and 'superstitious' (i.e. Catholic) books were burned. When his sister Mary succeeded to the throne it all happened again, though this time in reverse. But her reign will always be remembered for the burning of three men, bishops Hugh Latimer and Nicholas Ridley, and the former Archbishop of Canterbury, Thomas Cranmer. Their offence, that they were Protestants. All three were held in the Bocardo prison in Oxford, a chamber over the north gate. Latimer and Ridley were publicly burned on 16 October 1555 in the Broad. Cranmer was burned separately the following year. A simple cross set out in cobbles on the road marks the infamous spot: the Martyrs' Memorial at the end of St Giles was not the place of execution. Latimer's reported final words were 'Be of good comfort Master Ridley, and play the man: we shall this day light such a candle by God's grace in England, as shall never be put out.' With Elizabeth's accession to the throne the religious seesaw tipped again. Once more Oxford men suffered, though this time of the opposite persuasion. Some thirty Oxford priests, fellows of colleges, were executed as Catholics, including the Jesuit Edmund Campion, sometime student and fellow at St John's, who was hung, drawn and quartered for treason at Tyburn in 1581. In 1896 a Jesuit academic hall (in Brewer Street) was named in his honour, and he was belatedly canonised in 1970.

Two bizarre proposals for new colleges were put forward in the following century. The first, which appears to have had the blessing of Oliver Cromwell himself, was a scheme to strengthen the bonds between the English church and continental Protestant churches by founding a college. St Mary Hall (later absorbed into Oriel College) offered a suitable location. Although a draft document exists, it does not seem to have been taken forward. The second scheme, developed after the Restoration, was to refound the old Gloucester Hall as a college for Greek students in order to improve understanding between the English and Greek Orthodox churches. The plan was canvassed in both countries for several years and building repairs began in 1692. Although several Greek priests did study in Oxford, problems emerged and the college failed.

This reused vaulted gateway in New Inn Hall Street is all that can be seen of St Mary's Hall, *studium* for the Augustinian canons.

This simple cross in Broad Street marks the place of execution of bishops Cranmer, Latimer and Ridley.

Things to See

-The medieval colleges in the city centre are all gems.

-A reused vaulted gateway in New Inn Hall Street is all that can be seen of St Mary's Hall, *studium* for the Augustinian canons.

-A length of old wall contains a pedestrian gateway, the sole surviving fragment of the Cistercian Rewley Abbey. Cross Hythe Bridge and turn right down Upper Fisher Row, continue through the gate and along the footpath until you see the wall on your left.

-The terrace of cottage-like buildings in the main quad of Worcester College were the original accommodation of the Benedictine Gloucester College.

-Mob Quad, Merton College, was the first Oxford quadrangle.

-Stained glass in the choir of Merton College chapel by William of Thame was fitted 1310–11. In each panel kneeling images of the donor, Henry de Mamesfield, fellow and Chancellor, flank an angel (or saint).

-Christ Church Cathedral doubles as the chapel of Christ Church College. At its core is the twelfth-century chapel of the Augustinian priory.

-The cardinal's caps which decorate the south-west tower of Christ Church College are a reminder of Cardinal Wolsey's downfall.

-The wooden door of Archbishop Cranmer's cell in the Bocardo is preserved in the tower of St Michael's.

-A simple cross set out in cobbles in the roadway towards the west end of Broad Street marks the site of the martyrdom of bishops Cranmer, Latimer and Ridley.

6. War, Peace and Architecture

Following the stability of Elizabeth's reign, the seventeenth century started well for the university. Sir Thomas Bodley refurbished Duke Humfrey's Library and built the Schools Quadrangle. Other benefactors came forward with donations which added impressively to the university's and colleges' property portfolios. The Convocation House (closed to the public) was added to the west end of the Divinity School in 1634–37, with a library extension known as the 'Selden End' above.

Two new colleges were founded during James I's reign. Nicholas Wadham, a wealthy but childless West Country landowner, wished to found a college to perpetuate his memory. He died in 1609, but his energetic widow Dorothy drove the project forward. The former site of the Augustinian friars just outside the town wall was acquired in 1610, and the college that bears the family name was completed three years later. Its design around a quad is strongly influenced by Merton, but its Jacobean date is marked by a strong symmetry. The showpiece of Front Quad is a four-storey porch which slightly predates the grander porch in the Schools Quad at the Bodleian. Pembroke College was founded in 1624, nominally by James I but in reality by two little-known men, Thomas Teasdale, a merchant, and Richard Wightwick, a clergyman.

Samuel Fell, Dean of Christ Church, undertook the task of completing the great quadrangle, which had lain half built since Wolsey's downfall over a century earlier, very deliberately continuing the Tudor style of the original to create an architectural unity. Arguably his greatest achievement was the highly original and dramatic fan vaulted staircase vestibule to the hall.

This was also a period when many college chapels were 'beautified' under the influence of the university chancellor and high church archbishop William Laud, though this work was mostly undone in the 1640s and 1650s. Lincoln College chapel (1629–30) is the classic surviving Laudian college chapel. With its black-and-white pavement, rails, painted glass and ceiling, screen, organ, furnishings and plate, it provided a reverent setting for the sacred acts. The fantastical baroque south porch of the university church, St Mary the Virgin, with its pair of barley sugar twist columns, was added at this time at the expense of Laud's chaplain, Dr Morgan Owen.

This growing confidence was shattered as the mutual distrust of Crown and Parliament led in 1642 to civil war. The university was Royalist in sympathy while the town was more mixed. By August a militia of students and dons was being trained, though this small force was called away to join the King at Shrewsbury leaving the town undefended. Oxford's important strategic location on the Thames made it a valuable prize which the Parliamentary forces were quick to occupy. However, after disarming the town, seizing college silver and burning 'popish' books, they withdrew. After defeat at Edghill in October of that year, the Royalist forces in turn occupied Oxford and King Charles made

The striking Baroque south porch of St Mary the Virgin, High Street, was designed by Nicholas Stone in 1637.

it his capital for the remainder of the war. Defence was a priority. The two rivers could be flooded, leaving just the northern approach exposed. Redoubts protected the bridges while earthen fortifications were thrown up elsewhere to supplement the medieval town walls. This makeshift defence was upgraded when the leading military engineer of the age, Sir Bernard de Gomme, was engaged. A surviving plan thought to be by de Gomme shows that his defences were state-of-the-art, though how much was actually constructed is uncertain. Whatever was done impressed the Parliamentary commander Col Fairfax, who described it as 'having many strong bulwarks so regularly flanking one another, that nothing could be more exactly done; round about the line, both upon the bulwarks and upon the curtain, was strongly set with stormpoles; upon the outside of the ditch, round the line, it was strongly pallisadoed'. The Parliamentary forces dug in on Headington Hill in preparation for a long siege. The rest, as they say, is history. The King watched his support dwindle, and surrendered to the inevitable in June 1646. Parliament 'slighted' the defences so thoroughly to prevent their reuse that virtually nothing survives. A mound in New College garden might be an artillery platform though it later served as a garden feature. Slight traces of earthworks on Christ Church and Port Meadows may be further remnants.

The Civil War was a bad time for both the town and university, as it was for the whole kingdom. The town was occupied and besieged, so that normal commercial activity must have ceased; parts were destroyed, either by accident or deliberately, for example a fire burned down the Shambles while an area outside the defences was cleared to give a field of view. Hunger and overcrowding brought disease, with burials increasing six-fold. The university emptied as students and fellows sought safety elsewhere. Its wealth was seized and its buildings commandeered. The King and his entourage lodged at Christ Church; the Queen's household was at neighbouring Corpus Christi – and a private doorway made between them. Magdalen Grove became a park for field artillery. A cannon foundry was established in Christ Church and Gloucester Hall was used for munitions production. The royal mint moved into New Inn Hall and Lincoln College temporarily housed the exchequer. Soldiers were billeted in colleges and in houses around the town.

The university had backed the wrong side and at the conclusion of the war it was brought into line. As many as 190 (out of less than 350) fellows were replaced by those sympathetic to the regime, and dependable Puritan preachers were appointed. Student numbers remained low as government educational policy was more concerned with the new orthodoxy than with learning. College chapels suffered the same fate as parish churches across the land as men were once again dispatched with orders to destroy 'superstitious' images. Chapels which had been 'beautified' just a few years earlier under the influence of Laud were desecrated. The rare scheme of early fourteenth-century stained-glass windows in Merton College chapel may only have slipped under the radar by being whitewashed.

With the Restoration of the monarchy under Charles II, the university quickly regained its former confidence. Two buildings illustrate this very clearly – the Sheldonian Theatre and the old Ashmolean Museum, both in Broad Street.

The university was keen to create a new arena for its formal ceremonies. The result was the dual-purpose Sheldonian Theatre, intended as both a venue for granting degrees and a theatre for plays. The design was by Christopher Wren, at the time the Savilian Professor of Astronomy rather than the famous architect he was to become. Its classical model was the Theatre of Marcellus in Rome, hence the curved façade which faces the Broad. Wren's design had to be cut back to match the purse of the patron, Gilbert Sheldon, Archbishop of Canterbury, in who's honour the building was named. Sheldon eventually parted with £12,239 plus £2,000 to set up a maintenance fund. A classical theatre was open to the skies, a thing which was impossible in Oxford's climate, so a flat canvas ceiling was painted by Robert Streeter to create the appropriate illusion backed up by allegorical figures. When it was opened in 1669, the final university activities were transferred from St Mary's church where they had been performed for over 400 years.

The Ashmolean became the first purpose-built museum in Britain. It traces its origins to the extensive collection built up by the gardening dynasty of John Tradescant and his son John. This early style of museum was what is known as a gentleman's 'cabinet of curiosities', indiscriminately gathering together natural and man-made, ancient and modern objects. John the younger described it as 'those rarities and curiosities which my Father had sedulously collected'. It opened to the public at Lambeth (London), and the help of Elias Ashmole was enlisted to create a catalogue (published in 1656). In 1677 John the younger passed the collection via Ashmole to the university. As there was nowhere to display such a gift, a museum was constructed on the Broad next door to the Sheldonian and opened by the future James II on 21 May 1683. Surprisingly, its architect is uncertain, but may have been the master mason Thomas Wood. The building now houses the Museum of the History of Science.

The Sheldonian Theatre, the university's ceremonial heart, was built in 1663–69. The curved façade facing Broad Street reflects its classical model, the Theatre of Marcellus in Rome. The lantern was added in 1838.

The Old Ashmolean Museum was built in 1678–83 to house the collection presented by Elias Ashmole. It is now the Museum of the History of Science.

College chapels were restored following the desecrations of the Commonwealth period. One such is Trinity which, with ornate stucco work and carving in the style of Grinling Gibbons, was eulogised by Nikolaus Pevsner as 'one of the most perfect ensembles of the late C17 in the whole country'. The great architect Sir Christopher Wren was responsible for several college projects at this time. His final commission in Oxford was to complete the great gateway at Christ Church. Wolsey's original plan was adapted to take a bell, and the 7-ton Great Tom, which 150 years before had hung in the abbey church at Oseney, was recast and relocated. It first tolled the curfew on 29 May 1684.

The town also saw much building and rebuilding in the seventeenth century, both before and after the Civil War, though this is usually masked by later work. Often the basic structure is of timber with plaster infill: building in stone was reserved for higher budget college and church projects. Within the walls, several taverns include seventeenth-century work and are, of course, open to the public. The Mitre on the High Street has a range of c. 1630 raised over a medieval cellar; The Chequers, also in the High Street, includes seventeenth-century alterations. Many houses down narrow lanes have also avoided demolition. Outside the walls, many of the houses along St Giles hide a seventeenth-century core behind a later façade, for example the Eagle and Child inn, which was frequented by the Inklings including C. S. Lewis and J. R. R. Tolkien. Several older survivors are evidence that this part of the town was not levelled during the Civil War, and the White Horse Inn in Broad Street is another late sixteenth-/early seventeenth-century building. Many of the elegant houses along Holywell Street are also seventeenth century in date.

Patrons continued to seek glory in bricks and mortar. The most generous of eighteenth-century benefactors was Dr John Radcliffe, an eminent physician. On his death in 1714 he made a substantial bequest to University College, his old college. Other funds were left in trust and used to build the Radcliffe Camera, Radcliffe Infirmary, Radcliffe Observatory and the Oxford Lunatic Asylum. £40,000 was specifically for a library. The result was one of Oxford's iconic buildings, a classical cylinder topped by a dome. Housing was swept away to create space for the Radcliffe Camera, by James Gibbs, which was completed in 1749 and still serves its original purpose. The original Radcliffe Infirmary on the Woodstock Road has since been buried beneath later accretions; the hospital has moved out to Headington, where it still honours his name. The Radcliffe Observatory on the Woodstock Road has found a new use as part of Green College, appropriately a post-graduate college for medicine. Prior to this the *University Gazette* regularly announced, 'The Director of the University Observatory gives notice that on fine and clear Thursday evenings in the Michaelmas and Hilary terms between 8 and 10p.m. celestial objects will be shown through the telescope to members of the University and friends accompanying them.'

The University Press had been squeezed into spare corners in the Sheldonian Theatre for the previous thirty years. When the huge commercial success of the Earl of Clarendon's *History of the Great Rebellion* (published 1702–04) caught it by surprise, the profits from this book alone allowed the Press to consider new premises. The result was the Clarendon Building of 1711–15 to designs by Nicholas Hawksmoor, sometime assistant to both Sir Christopher Wren and Sir John Vanbrugh. Space remained tight, and in 1830 the Press moved to new purpose-built premises in Walton Street. Today this building gives the impression of being little more than a gateway to the treasures of Schools Quad and the Bodleian Library beyond.

Left: Solid seventeenth-century housing in Pembroke Street, built in 1641.

Below: The Eagle & Child, the seventeenth-century inn on St Giles, was a favourite of C. S. Lewis, J. R. R. Tolkein and their circle.

The Radcliffe Camera from All Souls College. This iconic building, a library, was funded from a huge bequest by Dr John Radcliffe. It was not completed until 1749.

The delightful Holywell Music Room was erected by public subscription in the 1740s as a concert venue, making it the oldest custom-built concert hall in Europe. It now provides facilities for the Faculty of Music and continues to be used for recitals.

During the quiet and prosperous years of the eighteenth century several colleges took the opportunity to remodel or build anew. The Front Quad at The Queen's was redesigned, presenting its screen and cupola-topped gatehouse to the High Street. Hawksmoor was engaged as architect for the new North Quad at All Souls with its pair of extraordinary Gothic towers. Peckwater and Canterbury Quads at Christ Church were designed by James Wyatt; he was also the architect of the Radcliffe Observatory.

If these were years of architectural splendour for the university, intellectual life was often dull. It became something of a 'finishing school' for wealthy young men who had no intention of taking a degree. It was not until 1928 that the majority of undergraduates were reading for honours. One gentleman commoner, James Harris (student in 1763–65), later earl of Malmesbury, said, 'The two years of my life I look back to as most unprofitably spent were those at Merton. The discipline of the University happened also at this particular time to be so lax, that a Gentleman Commoner was under no restraint and never called upon to attend either lectures, or chapel, or hall.' Edward Gibbon (Magdalen 1752), author of the weighty *Decline and Fall of the Roman Empire*, portrayed the university as 'sunk in port and prejudice, and almost completely indifferent to its educational mission' (*DNB*). He bitchily observed in his autobiography, 'the fellows of my time were decent, easy men ... their days were filled by ... the chapel and the hall, the coffee-house and the common-room, till they retired, weary and well satisfied, to a long slumber'.

In contrast to this picture of decadence, Oxford could produce a man like John Wesley. He won a scholarship at Christ Church, graduating in 1724, took holy orders and became

Above: Looking through the Clarendon Building archway towards Schools Quad and the Bodleian Library.

Left: The classical façade of the purpose-built Holywell Music Room of 1742–48.

North Quad, All Souls College, with its distinctive pair of towers, was built in a vaguely Gothic style in the 1720s to designs by Nicholas Hawksmoor.

North Quad, All Souls College, from the passage linking with Front Quad. The large sundial which dominates the Codrington Library was probably designed by Christopher Wren (as professor of astronomy) and later moved to its present position.

Edmund Halley (the astronomer, 1656–1742) built an observatory on the roof of this house in New College Lane. Despite the limited nature of science teaching in the seventeenth and eighteenth-century university, many eminent scientists were attracted to Oxford.

a fellow of Lincoln College. It appears to have been at this time that he began to explore spiritual discipline, reading a number of prominent authors. Soon he had gathered a group of like-minded friends and formed the Holy Club, an informal network of university men who met to study the Bible. He went on to preach all over the country, often in the open air, travelling thousands of miles on horseback. Wesley himself never intended to break with the Church of England: that step was forced upon his followers by prejudice and ridicule. For example, in 1768 six students were expelled from St Edmund Hall for being Methodist. 'Enthusiasm', whether religious or political, was a dirty word in eighteenth-century Britain.

Things to See
- The Sheldonian Theatre in Broad Street.
- Old Ashmolean Museum, now the Museum of the History of Science, next door to the Sheldonian.
- The fan-vaulted staircase vestibule to the hall in Christ Church College.
- Lincoln College chapel, a surviving Laudian design of c. 1630.
- Trinity College chapel, a showcase of the 1690s.
- Radcliffe Camera, still a library after 250 years (no public access).
- Eagle & Child, St Giles, a seventeenth-century inn and haunt of the Inklings.
- Lamb & Flag, St Giles, another seventeenth-century inn almost opposite.
- A plaque in New Inn Hall Street records both Wesley preaching and the site of the first Methodist meeting house in Oxford.

7. Towards the Modern University

As the nineteenth century dawned, Oxford continued to drag its feet. Latin continued to be the language of study, though this was to change. The Classics were believed to train the mind better than anything else and fit a gentleman for whatever he was to do in future. History was also emerging as a subject suitable for those who wished to become civil servants, and the curriculum was gradually broadening to embrace the sciences.

Oxford theologians shook the nation in the 1830s, in the process permanently changing the character of the Church of England. A group of Oxford men led by John Henry Newman, vicar of St Mary's, set out to renew the spiritual life of the Church and to prove its legitimate continuity with the early church. They started what became known as the Oxford Movement and promoted their views through a series of pamphlets named *Tracts for the Times*, for which reason they were also called Tractarians. The most controversial was *Tract XC* of 1839, Newman's innocuously entitled *Remarks on Certain Passages in the Thirty-Nine Articles*, which set out to minimise any difference between the Anglican and Catholic churches. The group's High Church practices were criticised by those who felt they were Catholics in all but name, then in 1845 Newman, their leader, was received into the Catholic Church, subsequently becoming a cardinal. However, the movement survived that dramatic justification of its critics.

Quite apart from its impact on the Church, Tractarianism left an enduring mark on Oxford in bricks and mortar. At the death of John Keble, a hugely influential member of the inner band, an appeal was launched to found a college. The result was the polychrome brick college in Parks Road which bears his name. It was built in 1868–82 to designs by William Butterfield and has continued to cause controversy as architectural fashions have changed. The chapel contains the famous painting of Christ as *The Light of the World* by Holman Hunt – or one of them as, in a fit of pique, the artist made a copy which hangs in St Paul's Cathedral! Another college was to follow. In 1884 Pusey House in St Giles was founded as a theological college to maintain the principles of the Oxford Movement and as a memorial to Edward Bouverie Pusey, another important advocate for the cause. However, the Tractarians were not universally acclaimed. Many felt that they had turned their back on the values of the Reformation and had dismissed their Anglican heritage. The Martyrs' Memorial, erected in 1841 to commemorate Cranmer, Latimer and Ridley, was a response to this unease and a direct challenge to the Tractarians – a reminder of what the English Reformation had cost in Oxford. It is modelled on an 'Eleanor cross', a series of monuments erected by the grieving Edward I to the memory of his queen, and it stands prominently at the end of St Giles rather than on the site of the martyrdoms in Broad Street. Ironically, Pusey House was later built almost opposite.

Meanwhile, concern was widely expressed that the universities were unaccountable, places of privilege and wealth which were failing to meet the needs of the nation. In

The Martyrs' Memorial, at the start of St Giles', was erected in 1841–43 to commemorate the Protestant bishops Cranmer, Latimer and Ridley; it was not their actual place of execution.

1850 a Royal Commission was appointed to inquire into the state, discipline, studies and revenues of the university and colleges of Oxford. Access, quality and relevance were all on the agenda. It concluded that the university was governed by too small a power base while colleges were too wealthy and independent, factors which were 'inimical' to academic and social progress. An Act of Parliament then imposed new constitutional measures, though these were not very far reaching. A further Royal Commission looked at financial issues. Although little concrete was achieved, Parliament had signaled its interest in higher education.

Another pivotal decision forced upon the university from the outside was the repeal of the Test Act in 1871. This removed the bar to non-Anglicans becoming members either as students or fellows, whether Catholic, Nonconformist or Jew. The first Catholic church in Oxford since the Reformation was a simple Jesuit chapel (now disused), built in 1794 in St Clement's. Then, with the abolition of the Test Act, Catholics were allowed back into the university. By the time the lavish St Aloysius on Woodstock Road was built in 1875, the position of Catholics in Oxford (and England) had completely changed and they could afford to be visible and flamboyant. Ironically, today the university's Catholic chaplaincy in Rose Place occupies a half-timbered building alleged to have been the palace of Bishop King, last abbot of Oseney and first bishop of Oxford – the bishop's tomb is still in the cathedral. The religious orders have also returned to the city. The Salesian Fathers arrived in Cowley in the 1880s to set up a school. Today Greyfriars, Campion Hall for the Society of Jesus, St Benet's Hall for the Benedictines of Ampleforth, and Blackfriars for the Dominicans all have the status of permanent private halls.

The former bishop's palace in Rose Place, opposite Christ Church War Memorial Garden, now houses the Catholic chaplaincy and a café. Its core dates from the sixteenth century, extended in the 1620s.

Museums represented a new approach to learning – hands-on and empirical rather than philosophical. The University Museum of Natural History on Parks Road was designed as both a museum and a space for science teaching: the first scientific laboratory space had been shoehorned into the basement of the Sheldonian Theatre. For once the university seems to have moved quickly, from a resolution in 1849 to construction in 1855–60. Internally, the building is a remarkable mix of Gothic forms with state-of-the-art materials – pointed arches of cast iron and glass. No opportunity to educate the visitor was missed. The capitals topping each pillar in the main court are carved with botanically correct plants, while the different rocks used in the pillars are identified. Today the museum is best known for its dinosaur skeletons and its dodo. A stuffed dodo, a flightless bird which has been extinct since the seventeenth century, was part of the original Tradescant-Ashmole donation – although sadly only the head and feet were saved when it was found to be decaying and are now displayed alongside a reconstruction. Appropriately, the museum was the venue in June 1860 for the defining debate between Samuel Wilberforce, Bishop of Oxford, and T. H. Huxley about the implications of Charles Darwin's book *Origin of Species* – a sculpture in the forecourt commemorates this. A museum extension was built in 1885 to house the Pitt-Rivers Museum, an eclectic anthropological collection assembled by General Pitt-Rivers and donated to the university. Its displays are still presented in the cluttered and confusing yet fascinating manner favoured by the General – almost a museum of museums.

On a different level, Thomas Howard, 2nd Earl of Arundel, had assembled an important collection of classical marble sculpture. The bulk of this formed a major donation to the university by his grandson, while a further gift was received in 1755. In the absence of a dedicated gallery, this material was displayed in the Bodleian Art Gallery together with the university's growing art collection. A more appropriate solution was sought, but it was not until 1845 that the collection could be moved to new galleries in Beaumont Street, designed in the Greek revival style by Charles Robert Cockerell. Only in 1894 was the general archaeological collection, the core of which was still the Tradescant collection donated by Elias Ashmole, transferred there to sit alongside the art and sculpture to create the Ashmolean Museum.

The late nineteenth century saw a renewed interest in founding colleges. After a gap of 250 years, punctuated solely by the refounding of Worcester College, Keble College was the first new men's college in 1870. Twenty years later, the two Nonconformist institutions of Manchester and Mansfield colleges relocated to Oxford, though without (at first) becoming part of the university. Hertford College fits into this story, and it has a chequered history. Founded before 1282 as Hart Hall, and with few endowments and a confined site at the junction of New College Lane and Catte Street, it managed to struggle on. In 1740 it was granted the status of a college, but its fortunes continued to decline until, in 1818, its street frontage collapsed due to disrepair. Its site was used to relocate another of the old academic halls, Magdalen Hall, which the much larger Magdalen College was finding an awkward neighbour. Its miracle of rebirth began in 1874 when the banker Thomas Baring made a large donation. Building work began and the name of Hertford College was resurrected. Today the picturesque Bridge of Sighs (fancifully named after the famous bridge in Venice), built just before the First World War, links its two quads across New College Lane.

But the real impetus came with the opening up of higher education for women. In 1866 women were first allowed to attend some lectures while separate classes were also

In the 1840s the university built a new museum in the Classical style to display its growing collection of sculpture and art works. The Ashmolean Museum was created in 1894 when the University's archaeological collections, including Ashmole's bequest, were transferred there.

organised for them, though it was not until the Sex Disqualification (Removal) Act of 1919 that they were admitted to full membership and were able to take the degree. The first two ladies' colleges to push forward the claim for equality of education were Lady Margaret Hall (1878) and Somerville (1879). A different type of institution was the Society of Home Students (1879), which provided oversight for young gentlewomen who felt it more appropriate to live quietly at home in Oxford while they studied. It was not until 1952 that the society became St Anne's College. St Hugh's Hall (1886) and St Hilda's Hall (1893), both later renamed colleges, were founded before the end of the century. Today every college admits both men and women – the last institution to do so was St Benet's Hall, a Benedictine foundation, in 2015.

The growth of the university continued into the twentieth century, though the first college to mention is an unusual case. The Delegacy for Non-Collegiate Students was

The Bridge of Sighs, Hertford College, which spans New College Lane, dates from immediately before the First World War.

Somerville College (founded 1879) on Woodstock Road was one of the first wave of womens' colleges.

formed in 1868 in response to the urgent need identified by the Royal Commission of 1852 to broaden access to the university. Colleges were seen to be expensive while a non-collegiate society offered a cheaper option for undergraduates. The delegacy developed into St Catherine's College in 1962, occupying thoroughly modern buildings. The cost of a university education continued to exclude many potential applicants. The first effective step towards broadening access came with the 1944 Education Act: tuition was now free and maintenance grants were available. This encouraged social mobility, primarily from the grammar schools. Today 'access' remains high on the agenda.

Although undergraduates remain the university's 'bread and butter', the balance has decisively tipped towards post-graduate study and research. In later life Viscount Nuffield became known as a philanthropist with an interest in educational and medical causes. In 1937 he founded Nuffield College, donating the site, the former basin of the Oxford Canal, plus £900,000. Given his background, Nuffield unsurprisingly wanted a college of engineering, but when the university held out for a graduate college of the social sciences he acquiesced. St Anthony's College (1948), Linacre College (1962), St Cross College (1965), and Green College (1979), followed. Wolfson College received its Royal Charter in 1981. Kellogg College (1990) provides for part-time graduate studies. In addition, undergraduate colleges have always accepted graduate students.

To cope with this growth, many new departments, laboratories and facilities have sprung up piecemeal. As an illustration, the tale of the Bodleian Library's constant hunger for space is unending. Thomas Bodley's original Library very quickly outgrew its accommodation – even his own will made provision for the extension. Some slight relief came when the Radcliffe Camera was used to house scientific books. Then, with the library stuffed to bursting, a separate new building was belatedly erected in the 1930s. (As a measure of resistance to change, the Bodleian had no electric light until 1929, which severely curtailed its opening hours.) The New Bodleian, just around the corner in Parks Road, was designed to hold five million volumes. Then, when yet another bookstore

The entrance to Nuffield College from New Road. Nuffield is a graduate college, founded in 1937 by Lord Nuffield, the motor manufacturer.

The audience gather in the classical-style open-air theatre on the roof of the Said Business School for a performance of *The Merchant of Venice* by the Creation Theatre Co. This newly built theatre offers an unusual summer venue. (© Clare Sargent)

was needed, it was carved out underground beneath Radcliffe Square. These sites were linked by a tunnel through which books were transported on a 1940s conveyor. Pressure on storage space inevitably continues to grow, and today roughly 80,000 new books and 78,000 serials are accessioned each year under the Copyright Act. Recently, deep storage has been built near Swindon to hold volumes which are seldom called. This released the book store under Radcliffe Square to be refurbished as a reading room over two floors, known as the Gladstone Link, with the old tunnel providing foot access for readers. Meanwhile, the New Bodleian has been transformed as the Weston Library.

The former Oxford Polytechnic became Oxford Brookes, Oxford's 'other' university, in 1992. Mention must also be made of Ruskin College, founded in 1899. Independent of the university, Ruskin continues to offer working people the opportunity of education to a university level.

Things to See
- Holman Hunt's *The Light of the World* in Keble College chapel.
- The University Museum of Natural History, famous for its dodo and dinosaurs.
- The Pitt-Rivers Museum, a fascinating ethnographic collection.
- The Ashmolean Museum has much to offer depending on your interests.
- Martyrs' Memorial at the head of St Giles'.
- The Bridge of Sighs, which spans New College Lane.
- Jacob Epstein's *Lazarus* in New College chapel.

8. A Regular Town

With the tourist focus on the university, it would be easy to forget that Oxford is a regular town – parallel universes, but with considerable overlap. It existed for perhaps half a millennium before the masters settled in its simple streets, serving as a market centre for the surrounding area, though its position at a major Thames crossing gave it a national as well as a purely local role. Writing in the 1930s, John Betjeman could still recognise the outlines of an ordinary market town, his 'Christminster' – a small country town with cathedral.

Medieval Oxford was primarily a market town like countless others, with stalls, small lock-up shops and workshops lining the main streets, a town of craftsmen and traders. At first the scholars simply represented welcome additional business, but gradually the tail came to wag the dog of civic life as the university clung tenaciously to the rights it gained following the riots of 1209 and 1355. As the wider role of the town declined, its prosperity became increasingly bound up in a love-hate relationship with its major client, the academic body.

The Covered Market was created by the civic authorities in 1772 to clear the streets of market stalls and barrows, and cattle were sold at Gloucester Green and later at Oxpens. Oxford's fair is known as St Giles' Fair, closing St Giles' to traffic for two days. This developed from a parish festival first mentioned in 1624, and is traditionally held on the Monday and Tuesday following the first Sunday after St Giles' Day (1 September). Its character has constantly changed, at times generating a reputation for drunkenness and violence. Today it is mainly a pleasure fair with rides and stalls for children and adults, and street vendors selling everything from roast chestnuts to clocks.

Oxford is a river town. The medieval Thames was a braided river, its course divided into numerous streams separated by watery islands. This water was a valuable resource, driving mills to process foodstuffs or to power small-scale industry. Oseney Abbey, on its island site, owned several, while the scant remains of a later incarnation of the Castle Mill can be seen in the shadow of St George's tower. The Trill Mill and Blackfriars Mill were on either side of St Aldate's. Today the Trill Mill Stream, in origin surely manmade, flows culveted and forgotten beneath the town to re-emerge on the edge of Christ Church Meadow.

River trade was important until the thirteenth century when the Thames became increasingly difficult to navigate above Henley. For example, at the request of the merchants of Oxford the monks of Abingdon Abbey cut the Swift Ditch to bypass their abbey mill and a difficult bend in the river. An eighteenth-century innovation revived the town's waterborne prosperity. This was the age of canals, when access to the inland waterways could make or break a town. Less than ten years after the Bridgewater Canal (the first canal in the world), a new canal was authorised by Parliament. The Oxford Canal, built by the great engineer James Brindley, snaked for 91 miles from its junction

Above: Magpie Lane and Wheatsheaf Passage preserve the lines of two of the many dark and narrow side streets which ran down from the main thoroughfares of the medieval town.

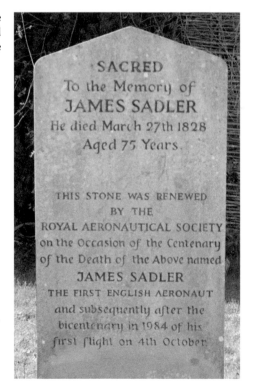

James Sadler was a remarkable Oxfordian. Born in 1753, son of a cook and confectioner, he went into the family business. He was an inquisitive young man, developing a career as an engineer, chemist and inventor. But his real passion was flight. On 4 October 1784 he made history by becoming the first Briton to fly, ascending to 3,600 feet in his home-made balloon. A plaque in Deadman's Walk marks the ascent. He made his forty-seventh ascent in 1815 aged sixty-two. He died in 1828 and was buried in the churchyard at St Peter-in-the-East.

A corner of the Covered Market. Colourful stalls sell a mixture of food, artisan and specialist goods.

Some of the collection of over 4,500 cut-off club ties in the Bear Inn, Bear Lane.

with the Coventry Canal, reaching Oxford and the Thames in 1790. Wharf facilities were built (some now beneath Nuffield College) where freight was transhipped from canal to river barges to continue its journey to London and the docks. The canal remained in low-level commercial use into the 1950s, ideal for bulky goods such as coal.

The Victorians were concerned about the spiritual and moral state of rootless wanderers such as bargemen and navvies. Consequently philanthropists paid for a floating chapel capable of accommodating 150 people, which was moored opposite the wharf on Upper Fishers Row. It was consecrated in 1839 by the bishop of Oxford, with the dual mission of serving as a bargemen's chapel on Sundays and a school for their children on weekdays. Inevitably it slowly decayed until one Sunday in 1868 it sank. The decision was taken to replace it with a hall built beside the canal on dry land in Hythe Bridge Street. The building still stands, but with the decline of the canals it has become a restaurant.

Right: The remains of the Castle Mill, once one of the main flour mills for the town, straddle the Castle Mill Stream. Behind, St George's Tower rises forbiddingly above the castle wall.

Below: Barges moored on the Oxford Canal.

The dominating presence of the river ensured there was a flourishing boatbuilding industry. In the early nineteenth century there were two boatbuilding firms, Thomas Hall and Isaac King, both with premises near Folly Bridge. The brothers John and Stephen Salter learned their trade in London before establishing their Oxford business in 1858 on the north bank of the Thames at No. 43½ St Aldate's. They soon bought out their rivals on their way to becoming perhaps the largest inland boatbuilder in the country. From the outset they made racing craft, which were often leased to crews, and built a variety of vessels, from college barges to lifeboats. In addition they kept a fleet of pleasure skiffs for hire. They ran a steam passenger service with links with GWR, and when that ceased to be commercial operated a private charter service. Salter's still runs river cruises in the season.

The next big technological development a town could not afford to miss out on was the railway. A Great Western Railway (GWR) station was opened just south of Folly Bridge in June 1844. This was the terminus until the line was extended to Banbury in 1850 and on to Birmingham 1852. In 1852 a new GWR passenger station was built on its present site in the Botley Road next to the LNWR station (now under the Said Business School). Grandpont station continued as a goods station until 1872: Marlborough Road follows the course of the old railway line.

After the river, the canal and the railway came the internal combustion engine and its great proponent, William Morris, manufacturer of the Morris Oxford. The Oxford we know today is as much a legacy of Morris as it is of the historic university. If he had not chosen the town as the site of his motor works and so triggered development, Oxford might still be a pocket-sized city like Wells (Somerset) with its cathedral and only 12,000 residents.

In 1874 another Oxford icon was born. Frank Cooper, then a grocer, began to market his wife's marmalade from his shop at No. 83 High Street. Cooper's Oxford Marmalade soon became a British breakfast tradition. In 1903 the business moved to a new purpose-built factory in Park End Street. The new premises were ideally located for distribution, just across the road from the GWR and LNWR stations. In the 1960s production was moved to a new factory before the firm was bought out – but the name was retained. The building in Park End Street, now renamed the Jam Factory, is an arts centre and restaurant.

Although Oxford has long held a reputation for privilege, one notorious drama of segregation was played out which had nothing to do with the university. In 1934 a developer outraged the nation by building 6-ft-high walls topped with spikes across Aldrich Road/Wentworth Road and Wolsey Road/Carlton Road to divide his new private housing from the council's neighbouring Cutteslowe estate. The council tenants were characterised as having been moved out from the slums, although in fact many were incomers taking the new skilled jobs created at Morris. The roads were even given different names on either side of the wall. The Cutteslowe Walls became a *cause célèbre*. Despite ongoing protests and various attempts at demolition, they stayed until 1959, a monument to social prejudice. A blue plaque in Aldrich Road now marks the place where the infamous wall once stood.

Folly Bridge from the riverside path beside Christ Church Meadow. The present bridge was built in 1836 and has since been widened. Folly Island sits in mid-stream.

Folly Bridge was freed from tolls in 1850. The former toll house is now a newsagent.

The former Morris Garage in Longwall Street where William Morris first began his car business before moving out to Temple Cowley.

Left: The wagon entrance into the factory where Cooper's Oxford Marmalade was made (now 'The Jam Factory') in Park End Street. It was purpose-built in 1903 for the world-famous brand.

Below: A blue plaque marks the line of the infamous Cutteslowe Wall.

Things to See
- The Covered Market, created in 1772, offers a tempting range of artisan and specialist shops.
- The current Folly Bridge was built in 1835 and freed from tolls in 1850. The former toll house is now a newsagent's shop.
- The Jam Factory, Park End Street, the former Cooper's Marmalade factory.
- The Morris Garage of 1910 in Longwall Street. Before moving production out to Temple Cowley, William Morris was based here.

9. Green Spaces

The centre of Oxford is blessed with green spaces. Its topography has ensured that the meadowlands beside its two rivers, which historically were prone to flooding, have remained unbuilt upon – the Port Meadow on one side, Christ Church Meadow and the University Parks on the other. Green spaces, which until the middle of the twentieth century defined the boundary of the town, now penetrate into its heart.

Port Meadow consists of 300 acres of unimproved common to the west of the town. Traditionally it was flooded and frozen in winter to provide skating for the youth. Grazing livestock was already the prerogative of the Freemen of Oxford as marked by the Domesday Book. This tranquil spot has also played its part in war. Faint earthworks may be the last vestiges of the Civil War defensive circuit, and it served as a military airfield before and during the First World War. A plaque on the old bridge at Wolvercote, overlooking the Meadow, records the deaths of lieutenants Bettington and Hotchkiss of the Royal Flying Corps in a training accident in 1912.

Livestock graze on Christ Church Meadow in the junction of the rivers Cherwell and Thames. Further north, the University Parks run beside the Cherwell. An island in the parks is known as Mesopotamia (named eruditely after 'the land between the two rivers', Tigris and Euphrates, also known as 'the cradle of civilisation'). The bridge was reputedly built as a job creation scheme in 1923 during the Depression.

Well-manicured college lawns and gardens provide hidden green spaces, often closed to non-members but perhaps glimpsed tantalisingly through a gateway or waving behind a high wall. The grandest is Magdalen College which has its own deer park, albeit a small one, emulating many an eighteenth-century country house. A herd of fallow deer graze there in the winter months, while in the spring the deer park is noted for its dancing crop of snake's head fritillaries. College and University sports fields are often tucked out of sight behind the rows of houses which line the main roads out of the centre. At an average of one per college, they must constitute a considerable acreage.

In 1621 Henry Lord Danvers acquired 5 acres on the bank of the Cherwell beside Magdalen Bridge for a physic garden, giving the plot a splendid entrance gateway and growing walls. Although extended, it inevitably remains a confined though remarkably varied site. Its original purpose was to cultivate medicinal plants: the Botanic Garden is its modern manifestation. The university also maintains the Harcourt Arboretum at Nuneham Courtenay.

The river and canal provide another change of pace from the crowd and bustle of the city. Each is shadowed by a towpath. In the case of the canal, the walker is quickly plunged into a tunnel of trees, while the river footpath offers wide views over meadows for much of its length. Just south of Donnington Bridge lies Iffley Meadows, maintained by the Berkshire, Buckinghamshire and Oxfordshire Wildlife Trust for its springtime display of 20–30,000 wild snake's head fritillaries.

Magdalen College tower seen from the river across Christ Church Meadow: an idyllic Oxford view.

Christ Church College and cathedral from War Memorial Garden.

A college cricket ground. Each college maintains its own sports ground.

The Botanic Garden was founded as a physic garden in 1621. The gateways were designed by Nicholas Stone.

Tourist punts and boats for hire at Magdalen Bridge. Most colleges have their own.

A springtime display. Snake's head fritillaries at Iffley Meadows.

Just a short walk from St Clement's are two public parks – really one split by a road. Headington Hill Hall was built in 1861for the Morrell family who were wealthy brewers in the town, but in less affluent times it is part of Brookes University. Its leafy grounds are open to the public as Headington Hill Park. The South Park, across the road, was bought from the Morrell Trustees by the Oxford Preservation Trust in 1932 – a pillar by the famous stone-carver Eric Gill commemorates acquisition. In the Morrells' days, the two halves of their gardens were linked by an iron bridge over the road.

For those who like to combine their nature with literature, the C. S. Lewis Nature Reserve lies on the northern edge of Oxford, just beyond the ring road (A4142). Drive up Kiln Lane and turn into Lewis Close, where there is parking. This woodland and pond belonged to the author and academic C. S. Lewis, and are now managed by the Berkshire, Buckinghamshire and Oxfordshire Wildlife Trust. It is a tranquil place in which to enjoy wildlife and recharge your batteries within a stone's throw of the noise and asphalt of the city.

Things to See
- College gardens, e.g. New College, which is enclosed by the town wall.
- Botanic Garden.
- Christ Church Meadow.
- The river – see Walk 4.

10. Oxford's Suburbs and Villages

Most of this book concentrates on a radius of less than a mile around Carfax. As recently as 1902–03 the Ordnance Survey map showed a small town tightly constrained between the Thames and Cherwell, with a northwards extension creeping towards Summertown and a second, southern suburb across Magdalen Bridge. Beyond that was Oxfordshire. The surrounding countryside was still a rolling landscape of farms, fields, hedges and streams. A satellite of small rural villages, not yet dormitory settlements, owed nothing to the neighbouring town other than as an occasional market for their produce. North and South Hinksey, Iffley, Cowley and Temple Cowley, Headington and Headington Quarry, Marston, Wolvercote, Binsey and Botley were all small communities, mostly still pursuing the agricultural lifestyle of their ancestors. There was as yet no hint of the sprawling urban growth of the interwar years.

In his autobiographical poem *Summoned by Bells*, John Betjeman records his prep school years in Oxford during the First World War when the war meant less to him than bicycles and homework, and William Morris was yet to transform Oxford into a manufacturing town.

The earliest suburbs were very close to the town, almost clinging to its walls. Housing spread from St Aldate's down to the river as land was reclaimed, while the district of St Thomas's was established by Oseney Abbey. St Giles and Holywell were medieval in origin but clearly moved upmarket in the seventeenth century when new houses were built. Further expansion was slow, while the poorer areas within the walls such as St Ebbe's became ever more crowded and squalid. Terraces of elegant late Georgian houses with wrought-iron balconies on Beaumont Street date from the 1820s, but once again these were just a stone's throw from the wall. In the nineteenth century the suburb over Magdalen Bridge in St Clement's became a middle-class residential area within easy walking distance of the town.

Jericho was an area of terraced working-class housing on the flood-prone northern fringes of the town, apparently named after the seventeenth-century Jericho House inn. Workers' housing sprang up to service the canal when it arrived in 1790. An ironworks provided more employment. Then the University Press moved to new premises in Walton Street in 1830, spurring further rapid development. In the nineteenth century the district had a reputation for poverty and poor drainage. Today these houses are more likely to be occupied by university staff or London commuters, or perhaps a bijou restaurant, than traditional labourers.

The first suburb to push beyond the immediate confines of the town ran northwards from St Giles towards Summertown along the Banbury and Woodstock Roads. This land was mostly part of the endowment of St John's College, which was looking for ways to increase its income. The scheme was to promote a development of large detached or semi-detached leasehold villas in generous grounds on which the college could levy ground rent. A grid of broad and leafy streets would create a desirable environment, and the church of St Philip and St James was erected to serve the new community. The scheme proved more problematic than expected and dragged on over several decades – though a college can afford to take the long view. Different models were attempted. Samuel Seckham, a speculative builder, laid out the exclusive Park Town Estate in the 1850s. This combined two crescents of Georgian-style housing around a central garden and some detached villas. A limited company was formed, but buyers were slow to come forward. Norham Gardens (1860s–70s) was another speculative development. On other occasions leasehold plots were sold at auction leaving the purchaser to design and build their own house. The results were often highly individual, combining Gothic, Italianate

Beaumont Street stands on the site of the old royal Beaumont Palace. Many of its Georgian terraced houses have elegant wrought-iron balconies.

One of the secluded crescents of the Park Town estate, laid out around a central garden in the 1850s.

and Classical features. Today many of the large and often forbidding houses, replete with huge stained-glass windows and romantic turrets, which line the Banbury Road and its side roads serve as university departments or student accommodation, or are perhaps subdivided into flats.

A working-class development was grudgingly laid out as far as possible from this select neighbourhood of Gothic fantasies, on the site of Tagg's Gardens, a former nursery garden the west side of the Woodstock Road which connected with the Jericho estate. Once again the building work was let to speculative builders. Amusingly, the two communities were expected to share the new parish church of St Philip and St James.

This picture began to change when William Morris (ennobled as Viscount Nuffield) decided to locate his new car factory at Temple Cowley. The young William Morris learned his trade with a bicycle manufacturer in St Giles before setting up his own cycle repair business at the tender age of sixteen. Soon he experimented making motorbikes, progressing to motor cars in 1912. In 1914 he took a lease on a former military training college and began production proper after the war. He aimed at the popular market with his own design, the Morris Oxford, and his commercial success was down to a combination of volume production, low price and mechanical reliability. Morris paid good wages and built company housing, attracting skilled labour from the Midlands. By 1939 the works was employing around 2,250 people and has grown strongly since.

The ancient villages of the surrounding countryside have almost been overwhelmed, but they can still be traced within the spreading suburbs. One of the first to be absorbed was the early manor of Holywell, swallowed up by the growing town in the Middle Ages. The manor house and church of St Cross standing incongruously on the corner of St Cross and Manor Roads hint at an early existence. Other settlements or manors mentioned in the Domesday Book, at Cowley, Headington, Iffley, Seacourt and Wolvercote, have all hung on to varying extents.

Iffley is best approached on foot from the river. Cross Iffley Lock and wend your way up leafy village lanes, past thatch and old buildings, perhaps pausing at the village inn. Then on to St Mary's church, a magnificent gem dating from the 1170s. The west and south doorways are ornately Romanesque, with zigzag and animal head decoration, and inside it remains evocative. Adjoining the churchyard, the rambling rectory has served as the priest's house since the church was built. It feels generations away from neighbouring Cowley or the city centre.

Temple Cowley was chosen by William Morris as the site for his car works, and manufacturing success has not treated Cowley kindly. Today it is best known for its state-of-the-art BMW and mini works. There is virtually nothing before 1850. St James was the old parish church; although it was largely remodelled by G. E. Street in the 1860s, it is at heart still a medieval building. St Alban, Charles Street, was only built in 1933 but its sequence of the Stations of the Cross was carved by Eric Gill. For those interested in family history, the Oxfordshire History Centre is housed in the former St Luke's church on Temple Road.

Headington, conveniently close to the town, was the source of much of the raw material of Oxford, and the settlement of Headington Quarry grew up to service the need. Headington stone is a form of limestone known as Coral Rag, and its use first appears

Holywell manor house and the former St Cross church on the corner of St Cross Road and Manor Road. This was the heart of the ancient manor of Holywell.

The Romanesque church of St Mary, Iffley.

This is a deceptive scene! The former village church of St James set within its leafy graveyard complete with eighteenth-century headstones is tucked behind a multi-storey car park.

in university records with the building of New College bell tower in 1396–67. The last quarries were still being worked into the early years of the twentieth century. Over that span of time a lot of earth and rock was moved, so that the village grew up on a jumble of old quarries and waste heaps with road names such as Quarry Road and Quarry Hollow. Parts of the old quarries survive as public parks. It was at Headington Quarry that Cecil Sharp, a key figure in the revival of English folk dance, first saw traditional morris dancing in 1899 where its final vestiges were still clinging on.

Today Headington is a suburb of hospitals. At the time of the Domesday Book it was a royal manor, out of which the upstart *burh* of Oxford had been carved. St Andrew, with its chancel arch of 1160 carved in Romanesque zigzag, was the parish church of old Headington. A run of stone cottages opposite the church and some later Victorian brick terraces form a small oasis amid endless housing estates.

The heart of Old Marston remains a pretty village of cottages and stone houses. A plaque on the aptly named Cromwell House records that it was there that the peace treaty between the Royalist and Parliamentary forces was hammered out in 1646. The medieval church of St Nicholas sits comfortably in its old graveyard.

Wolvercote was already an ancient settlement when it was mentioned in the Domesday Book. Geoffrey of Monmouth wrote his *History of the Kings of Britain* in the twelfth century. He identified a tyrannical King Mempricius, who supposedly ruled Britain before the Roman conquest. This unpleasant character who slaughtered his way to power received his just desserts when he was torn apart by wolves while out hunting. Tradition suggested that this event took place at Wolvercote – but that sounds like a medieval attempt to derive the place name from a 'historical' character. More rigorous modern research suggests the name originally meant 'cot [settlement] of Wulfgar's people', Wulfgar presumably being an early Saxon landowner with a number of dependants.

Just across the Thames from Wolvercote are the ruins of the Benedictine nunnery of Godstow, founded in 1133. It has an unhappy royal association in the story of the love affair between Henry II and Rosamund Clifford, 'Fair Rosamund', much of which was probably conducted at Woodstock Palace (near Blenheim) with Oxford a staging post on the way. Legend tells that Henry's queen Eleanor arranged for the death of her lovely rival – poison is one suggestion. What is certain is that Henry grieved deeply over his loss. Rosamund was buried at Godstow nunnery, not far from Oxford, and the king made the nunnery numerous valuable gifts in her memory. By a strange twist of fate, she became a romantic figure and her tomb in front of the high altar drew pilgrims. When bishop Hugh of Lincoln visited in 1191 he was horrified at what he saw as the sacrilegious honouring of a strumpet, and ordered her body to be exhumed and reburied outside the church. Rosamund's grave in the churchyard was still marked (and visited) in the sixteenth century.

As you drive into Oxford along the Botley Road, spare a thought for the small agricultural settlement of Seacourt. This insignificant spot was mentioned in the Domesday Book. When the bypass (A34) was cut through the site in the 1950s, the opportunity was taken to excavate. The location is naturally damp. It appears that the village streets and yards were metalled to counter increasingly marshy conditions before the settlement was finally abandoned sometime in the mid-fourteenth century; its forlorn church collapsed a century later. Today its name is perpetuated in a car park!

The small Victorian church of Holy Trinity, Headington Quarry, is hidden away. C. S. Lewis is buried in the churchyard.

A row of stone cottages and the village pub face the churchyard across the main street of old Headington.

A quiet corner in Old Marston.

Above: A thatched cottage in Wolvercote.

Right: The ruins of Godstow Abbey, the twelfth-century Benedictine nunnery where the 'Fair Rosamund', mistress to Henry II, was buried.

Binsey is a tiny and astonishingly rural settlement of a few old cottages, a farm and a well-known inn hidden away among water meadows behind Botley Road. It was once famous by association with St Frideswide who reputedly created a miraculous well there. St Margaret's well had curative powers and was a place of pilgrimage; it still visited today. Binsey is also notable as Nicholas Breakspear, the only English pope (as Adrian IV), was priest there around 1125–30. He would have officiated in the twelftth-century church of St Margaret, which is still lit by candles, and would have known the well.

For completeness, mention must be made of North and South Hinksey. Both villages are to the west of the Thames so are interlopers which were historically in Berkshire. Both lie outside the city boundary but are squeezed within the circuit of the bypass; North Hinksey has been captured by the estates of Botley, while South Hinksey stands aloof. Both have a church of St Lawrence. That at North Hinksey has a Norman doorway, while that at South Hinksey is thirteenth century with an airy Georgian chancel. The parish of North Hinksey was the source of water for the Conduit in Carfax.

Things to See
- The following chapter includes a tour of the villages.

St Margaret's well, Binsey. Both St Frideswide and the English Pope Adrian IV knew this healing well behind St Margaret's church.

11. Four Walks and a Drive

1. Heart of the University

This walk will introduce some key university buildings as well as a sample of colleges.

1) Start on the High Street outside the porch of the church of St Mary the Virgin. This is the university church and was for many years the venue for many university meetings and activities.

2) Head down hill, turning left into Catte Street. The college on your right is All Souls: look through the ornate iron gate into the eighteenth-century North Quad designed by Nicholas Hawksmoor.

3) The pedestrianised street opens out into Radcliffe Square, with the Radcliffe Camera in its centre.

4) As you leave the square on the opposite side, the college on your right is Hertford. Admire the Bridge of Sighs which spans New College Lane.

5) On your left, go up the steps and through the gate in the railings. You have entered Clarendon Quad. On your right is the Clarendon Building, built with the profits from Lord Clarendon's *History*.

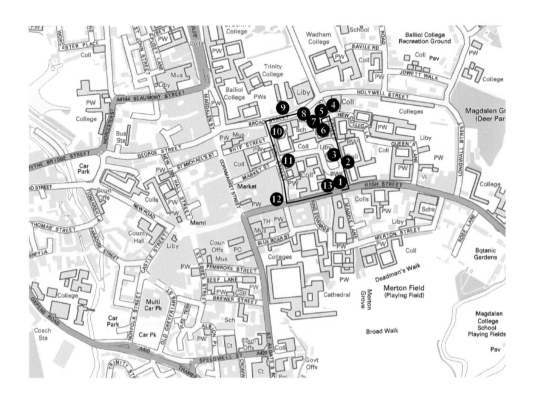

Left: The university's first building was the Congregation House, attached to the north side of St Mary's church, where the medieval regent masters met to conduct official business. The east end of the Congregation House is seen here from Catte Street.

Below: A railing defines a semicircular forecourt around the Sheldonian Theatre. Its piers are topped by busts of Roman Emperors; they were renewed in the 1970s.

6) Go through the passage on your left into Schools Quad. Notice the modest entrance to the Divinity School and Bodleian Library. The names of the schools or faculties are painted over the doorways.

7) Retrace your steps through the passageway to Clarendon Quad. On your left is the Sheldonian Theatre, the university's ceremonial venue.

8) Go through the gate in the railings in front of the Sheldonian into Broad Street and turn left. The next building on the left is the Old Ashmolean Museum, the first purpose-built museum in Britain; it now houses the Museum of the History of Science.
9) Continue along the Broad, which follows the line of the ditch which ran outside the town wall.
10) Turn left into Turl Street. The college on your left is Exeter, founded 1314.
11) Then Lincoln College, founded 1427.
12) As Turl Street reaches the High, the Mitre Inn is on one corner and All Saints' church on the other. The church is now the library of Lincoln College.
13) Return to St Mary's church. If you have the energy, the tower is open and gives impressive views over the town centre.

2. Circuit of the Town Wall

This walk follows the circuit of the town wall, although for most of the distance no trace can be seen above ground.

1) Starting at the castle mound, turn right up New Road.
2) Enter Bulwarks Lane, the first alley on the left. Continue along this alley, which runs behind New Inn Hall Street.
3) Turn right into a short alley which emerges in George Street, opposite the Corn Exchange (now Old Fire Station).
4) Right up George Street to the crossroads with Cornmarket. St Michael's church, the tower of which formed part of the town gate, is a short distance to your right.

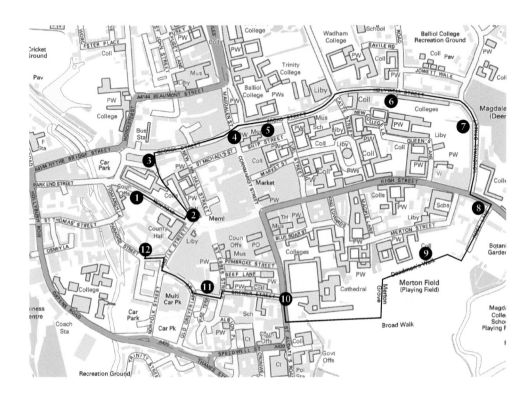

5) Cross into Broad Street, which follows the line of the town ditch. Parts of the wall are preserved in property boundaries behind the shops on your right. Its foundations have been seen beneath the quadrangle between the Clarendon Building and Schools Quad.

6) At the crossroads, continue straight ahead into Holywell Street. A good section of the town wall forms the garden perimeter of New College, behind the houses on your right, but this requires a detour to visit.

7) Turn right into Longwall Street. Once again, the wall ran behind the properties on your right – the castellated wall on the opposite side of the street is the perimeter of Magdalen College and not the town wall.

8) Cross the High Street and turn right into Rose Lane. At this point the wall is some way to your right.

9) Through the anti-bicycle gate and follow Deadman's Walk to the right. After the first bend, the wall is at last the town wall and the path diverts around a bastion. At the next bend the wall leaves the path and continues across Christ Church gardens towards the cathedral.

10) Continue past Christ Church and cross St Aldate's into Brewer Street; on your right, the boundary wall of Pembroke College follows the line. At the end of this lane is a plaque marking the position of the former town gate called Littlegate.

11) Cross into Turn Again Lane and continue straight along Old Greyfriars Street to Castle Street.

12) Cross over and follow Paradise Street to the gateway into the Castle complex.

A section of the old town wall running alongside Deadman Walk forms the boundary of Merton College garden.

3. Museums Walk

This route passes four of the university's more important museums. You may wish to allow time to explore them.

1) Start at the Tower of St Michael's church in Cornmarket and walk north into St Giles.
2) The church on the island just outside the line of the old town wall is the medieval St Mary Magdalen.
3) The Martyrs' Memorial, erected in 1841–43 to commemorate the execution of bishops Cranmer, Latimer and Ridley in 1555–56.
4) The first college on your right is Balliol, founded 1282, *alma mater* of Dorothy Sayers' fictional detective Lord Peter Wimsey.
5) On the corner of Beaumont Street is the Classical façade of the Ashmolean Museum. Its treasures are too numerous to mention.
6) On your right, the next college is St John's, founded 1555.
7) A little further on the left, the Eagle and Child tavern was a haunt of the Inklings.
8) In the fork between the Woodstock and Banbury Roads and dominating your walk so far is St Giles' church, founded in the twelfth century to serve the growing extra-mural community.
9) Turn right down Keble Road, with the patterned brickwork of Keble College, founded 1870, on your right hand.
10) Cross Parks Road and the grassy forecourt to the University Museum of Natural History. Its treasures include a dodo and various huge dinosaurs.
11) Do not miss the Pitt-Rivers Museum, the entrance to which is well hidden on the far side of the main exhibition hall.

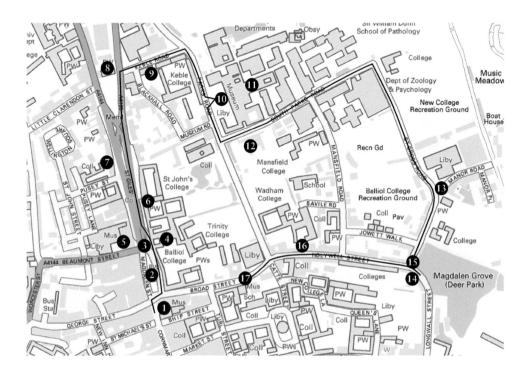

A cast of the skeleton of Tyrannosaurus Rex dominates the main hall of the University Museum of Natural History.

12) Leaving the museum, turn left and left again up South Parks Road. On your right is Rhodes House, centre for Rhodes visiting scholars. It was established under the will of Cecil Rhodes (died 1902), after whom Northern and Southern Rhodesia (Zambia and Zimbabwe) were named.

13) Follow the road to the right along St Cross Road. At the junction with Manor Road, Holywell Manor and the former St Cross church make a village-like grouping close to the heart of the city.

14) When the road bends sharply to the left into Longwall Street, take a few paces to admire William Morris's first factory for cars and motorbikes.

15) Retrace your steps to the junction with Holywell Street. A plaque on a wall to your left commemorates the execution of four Catholic priests in 1589.

16) Enjoy the seventeenth and eighteenth-century house frontages as you continue down Holywell Street, one of Oxford's more beautiful streets. On your left is Bath Place, a seventeenth-century court of a type which was once common (in most towns). On the right notice the Classical façade of the Georgian Holywell Music Rooms, the oldest purpose-built concert venue in England.

17) The walk ends in Broad Street, outside the Museum of the History of Science (the original Ashmolean Museum).

Bath Place off Holywell Street is a picturesque court of seventeenth- and eighteenth-century buildings. Such courts or alleys were once common in crowded towns.

4. Riverside Stroll

The towpath which follows the right bank of the Thames as far as the city boundary and beyond, is part of the Thames Path National Trail. The Boat Race is synonymous with Oxford (and Cambridge), and you are almost guaranteed to see eights or sculls practising on the river. This is a linear walk, so be prepared to retrace your steps (unless you arrange to be picked up either at Donnington Bridge or in Iffley village).

1) Walk down St Aldate's and cross Folly Bridge. Immediately over the bridge turn left down the footpath posted Thames Path.

2) On the opposite bank, Christ Church Meadow is followed by a run of college boat houses. These end where the Cherwell joins the Thames.

3) For the next ½ mile the river is lined by trees, meadows and leafy playing fields.

4) A few boat houses line the opposite bank on either side of Donnington Bridge, a road link across the river.

5) In a further ½ mile the walk ends at Iffley Lock. The river runs through fields; the first on this bank is Iffley Meadows nature reserve. Next, the Isis Farmhouse offers a chance of refreshment (check opening hours).

6) From Iffley Lock there is an opportunity to walk up leafy lanes to Iffley village.

7) Retrace your steps.

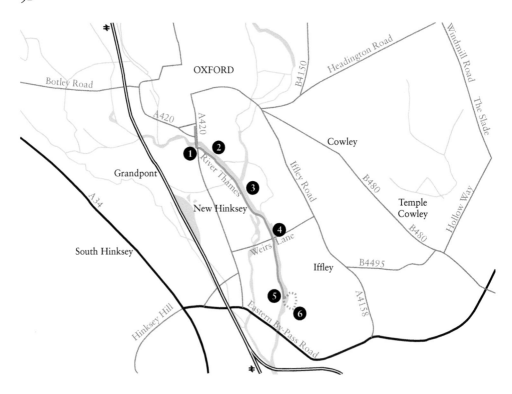

The river continues to play a large part in the life of many undergraduates, and rowing remains a major sport within the university. Each college owns or shares a boathouse.

A distant prospect of Iffley village from Iffley lock on the Thames.

5. Drive: Oxford Villages

For those with a car and time to explore, the old villages of Oxford repay the hunt. This is described as a circular tour, beginning at the A34/A420 roundabout at the head of Botley Road and ending back in the Botley Road.

1) First, **Iffley**. Follow the A34 south towards Abingdon, turning left onto the Southern Bypass (A423). Cross two roundabouts, keeping on the bypass. At the third roundabout, turn left into Oxford Road. After ¾ mile turn left into Church Way. Follow this road into the heart of **Iffley** where it forms a loop around Church Way and Mill Lane. This looks like a typical Cotswold village, with its cottages and occasional thatch. But the gem of national importance is St Mary's church which is a classic of the late twelfth century. Externally, its west and south doorways and the windows above are richly decorated. Inside, all is atmospheric. The core of the old rectory which backs onto the churchyard is almost as old as the church (and can be hired for holidays). If you have time, stroll down to the Thames at Iffley Lock.

2) Next, **Cowley**. Retrace your steps to the Oxford Road. Turn right and left into Church Cowley Road. This does not look encouraging, but turn right up the side of the multi-storey car park into Beauchamp Lane. Tucked away from the surrounding development is a forgotten fragment of rural **Cowley**. Drive between old stone walls. On your left, a terrace of traditional stone cottages. Opposite, the medieval church of St James still standing in its ancient churchyard. These scraps give a hint of the tranquillity that prevailed here before William Morris.

3) Back to Church Cowley Road. Turn right past the Templars Square Shopping Centre. Right again at the traffic lights onto (another) Oxford Road and immediately left into Hollow Way. In around ¾ mile bear left onto The Slade. Cross the roundabout into Windmill Road, then third right into Margaret Road. At the end of this road, thread your way slowly along Quarry Hollow, the dips and bends reflecting centuries of stone quarrying. This is **Headington Quarry**. The Victorian church of Holy Trinity is well hidden. When Quarry Hollow is about to join the bypass, turn right past The Six Bells into Spring Lane. C. S. Lewis is buried in the churchyard and the church has a Narnia window in his memory.

4) On to old **Headington**. Turn left onto the bypass and left again towards the city centre at the roundabout. At the lights past Bury Knowle Park, turn right into Old High Street. The medieval church of St Andrew boasts a Norman chancel arch. A couple of streets of old village houses make a very pleasing composition. This is **Headington** before the hospitals.

5) It is easiest to return to London Road and turn right towards the city. Right again at the lights into Headley Way, pass the John Radcliffe Hospital and turn right into Marsh Lane at the second of a pair of roundabouts. As you leave the built-up area, bear left as if for the bypass, but quickly turn left again for **Old Marston**. It was here, at Cromwell House, in May–June 1646, that King Charles I's surrender to Parliament was negotiated. **Old Marston** is another classic village overtaken by suburbia which provides a haven of peace from the rush all around. Traces of a wall painting have been revealed over the chancel arch in the church of St Nicholas, while its Jacobean pulpit was there before Cromwell and King Charles. The riverside Victoria Arms is well hidden.

6) Moving on to **Wolvercote**. Return down Elsfield Road, left onto the bypass slip road and join the Northern By-pass. Cross a roundabout, and at the second (major) roundabout take the second exit into Godstow Road, a minor road. **Wolvercote** is divided in two by a bridge over the Oxford Canal and railway, which makes it a difficult village to negotiate. Take the first left into Mere Road and right at the end. St Peter's church was rebuilt by the Victorians, but its fourteenth-century tower was retained. Make your way back to Godstow Road and cross the traffic-light-controlled bridge. Continue through the other half of the village which somehow manages to retain something of its rural origins. This road leaves the village via another bridge – we are down on the floodplain. The expanse of the Port Meadow opens up on your left: by Domesday Book this was already a common for the freemen of Oxford. At the riverside Trout Inn is yet another, older bridge, this time single track. The scant ruins of **Godstow Abbey**, the Benedictine nunnery where 'Fair Rosamund' was buried, are now grazed by sheep.

7) The next part of the tour leaves the boundaries of Oxford and crosses the bypass. Follow the road through Wytham (a pretty village about which nothing will be said), and eventually join the A420 back into Oxford. Take care not to be siphoned onto the A34 heading north! Once on the A420, cross the roundabout over the A34 and proceed down the Botley Road.

8) The final destination is **Binsey**. Pass the turning for Seacourt park & ride. Half a mile further towards the centre, turn left into Binsey Lane – it is posted as a dead end, but holds a secret. This quickly becomes a true country lane. **Binsey** comes as a surprise,

a rural village within the Oxford conurbation. A handful of ancient cottages cluster around a green, and the seventeenth-century Perch Inn is another of Oxford's hidden delights. The single track road ends in a farm gate and the tiny church of St Margaret. St Frideswide's miraculous well is behind the church. Stand here and watch sheep grazing as they did in the Saint's day, while traffic on the bypass thunders past a couple of fields away: is this a metaphor for modern Oxford?

Further Reading

The following titles will allow the reader to explore further.

Andrews, C. & D Huelin, *Oxford: introduction and guide* (Chris Andrews Pubs: Oxford, 1999 (revised edition).

Aston, T. H. (ed.), *The History of the University of Oxford*, 8 vols (Clarendon Pr: Oxford, 1984–2000).

Betjeman, John, *An Oxford University Chest* (Oxford University Press: Oxford, 1938 (reprinted 1979).

Blair, J., *Anglo-Saxon Oxfordshire* (Sutton Pub: Stroud, 1994).

Chance, E., *et al*, 'Medieval Oxford', in Crossley, A. & Elrington, C. R. (editors), *A History of the County of Oxford: Volume 4, the City of Oxford*, 3-73 (Inst Historical Research: London, 1979). Available online at http://www.british-history.ac.uk/vch/oxon/vol4/pp3–73 [accessed May–June 2015]

Dodd, A., *Oxford Before the University: the late Saxon and Norman archaeology of the Thames crossing, the defences and the town* (Oxford Archaeology, monogr 17, 2003).

Evans, G. R., *The University of Oxford: a new history* (I B Tauris: London, 2013).

Hall, M, *Oxford* (The Pevensey Press: Cambridge, 1987 (revised edition).

Hinchcliffe, T, *North Oxford* (Yale University Press, 1992).

Martin, G. H. & Highfield, J. R. L., *A History of Merton College, Oxford* (Oxford University Press: Oxford, 1997).

Morris, Jan, *Oxford* (Oxford University Press: Oxford, 1965 (reprinted 1987).

Oxford Dictionary of National Biography (available online at *http://www.oxforddnb.com/ public/index-content.html*).

Sherwood, J. & Pevsner, N., *The Buildings of England: Oxfordshire* (Penguin: London, 1974).

In addition, histories of individual colleges are in print and many colleges publish a guidebook.